T0039124

COMPUTER SCIENCE, TECHNOLOGY AND APPLICATIONS

AUCTION THEORY
FOR TELECOMS

COMPUTER SCIENCE, TECHNOLOGY AND APPLICATIONS

Additional books in this series can be found on Nova's website under the Series tab.

Additional E-books in this series can be found on Nova's website under the E-books tab.

COMPUTER NETWORKS

Additional books in this series can be found on Nova's website under the Series tab.

Additional E-books in this series can be found on Nova's website under the E-books tab.

COMPUTER SCIENCE, TECHNOLOGY AND APPLICATIONS

AUCTION THEORY FOR TELECOMS

MANOS DRAMITINOS

Nova Science Publishers, Inc.
New York

Library of Congress Cataloging-in-Publication Data

Dramitinos, Manos.
 Auction theory for telecoms / Manos Dramitinos.
   p. cm.
 Includes index.
 ISBN 978-1-61324-646-7 (hardcover)
 1. Auctions. 2. Electronic commerce. 3. Wireless communication systems. 4. Mobile communication systems. 5. Data compression (Telecommunication) I. Title.
 HF5476.D73 2011
 384.5'3--dc23
                                    2011014218

Published by Nova Science Publishers, Inc. ✛ New York

CONTENTS

PREFACE

The impressive growth of the Internet over the past years has resulted in constantly increasing demand for bandwidth. Hence, there is an increasing interest in new dynamic bandwidth trading mechanisms and more efficient ways of managing and charging the network resources. Also, the tremendous growth of wireless networks, including the cellular networks, combined with the increasing demand for services, has resulted in increasing demand for the reservation of spectrum; the spectrum is required in order for these networks to provide 2nd (GSM), 2,5 (GPRS) and 3rd (UMTS) generation services. This book both is an overview of the state of the art of the applications of auction mechanisms in the telecoms sector and provides a guideline for researchers working in the field of mechanism design and network economics.

The spectrum of the Radio Access Network is a scarce resource for the wireless networks. At the same time, the increasingly popular 3G services are extremely more demanding in terms of resource utilization than those of the 2G networks: Multimedia messages (MMS) replace the short text messages (SMS), while voice calls must still be accommodated along with data (e.g. photo, video, file transfers) services of much higher data rates. Moreover, the duration of these services is orders of magnitude greater than that of the network slots where the network resources are allocated (e.g. the duration of a UMTS frame is 10 msec).

The future convergence of the aforementioned technologies with other mobile network technologies and the potential introduction of multicast services also contribute to the dynamic nature of the telecommunications environment. Finally, this trend is further enhanced by the emergence of new technologies such as the Grid, Service Oriented Architectures and Software on Demand that require both virtualization and innovative resource allocation and management mechanisms.

This suggests that new resource allocation and charging mechanisms are needed in this dynamic context. To this end, *auctions* appear to be the proper trading mechanism. Auction mechanisms are very popular in such dynamic economic environments, since they provide a simple, fast and transparent means of determining the price of the goods that are to be sold. The most prominent and successful example of applying auctions in the telecoms sector is by far the Simultaneous Multiple Round (also referred to as FCC-type) auction, which was used by the Federal Communications Commission (FCC) of the United States of America to allocate radio spectrum to wireless service providers.

This book focuses on the use of auctions for resource allocation in communication networks and the telecoms industry in general. Following the Introduction (Chapter 1), the minimum required background from auction theory is presented (Chapters 2 and 3). Subsequently, the Simultaneous Ascending Auction - commonly referred to as the Simultaneous Multiple Round auction or FCC(-type) auction - which was used in the United States of America for the allocation of spectrum licenses to wireless telecom providers is presented. The European spectrum auctions are also discussed and the pros and cons of the various auction designs adopted at various countries, as well as the market conditions motivating some of these auction mechanisms' design decisions, are also overviewed (Chapter 5). Some other notable applications of auction theory in electronic markets are also presented (Chapter 6). Furthermore, this book addresses how auction theory can (and should not) be applied in the context of Grid and cloud computing (Chapter 7). Then, this book presents some interesting research topics where auctions can serve as the means of allocating the resources of both fixed-topology (Chapter 8) and wireless networks (Chapter 9) for competing unicast and multicast sessions in a both fair and economically efficient way. The book concludes with some final remarks (Chapter 10).

Overall, this book is both an overview of the state of the art of the applications of auction mechanisms in the telecoms sector and provides a guideline for researchers working in the field of mechanism design and network economics. This book is not intended to be a formal presentation of auction theory or a collection of auction papers. Also it is not limited to focusing on combinatorial auctions or just the FCC auction design but presents a variety of mechanisms and applications. Furthermore, for most of the research issues presented combinatorial auctions, despite their multiple merits in other contexts, simply do not work due to the problems' exponential complexity (the respective resource allocation problems are well-known NP-hard problems). Therefore, this book is more general and can serve as both an overview and introduction to how auction theory can be used in the telecoms sector. It is not an auction theory economics textbook. This book has a broader audience and can be easily read by non-experts who are interested in exploring the field. It is also very useful for non-economics students who need a reference to the basic auction mechanism design issues and the applications of auction theory to network resource allocation problems.

To Absent Friends

Chapter 1

INTRODUCTION

ABSTRACT

The presentation of this chapter begins with an overview of the modern telecoms environment. The major recent trends in telecoms driven both by the emerging technologies and the new business models of the telecoms sector are overviewed. Subsequently, a brief overview of the theory and the applications of auctions are provided. The criteria used for the assessment and evaluation of the various auction designs are briefly presented. Subsequently, this chapter provides a brief introduction to economics and auction theory. In particular, some fundamental concepts from economics are initially presented; the respective discussion and mathematical notation is intentionally kept to a minimum. However, the presentation of these concepts in an intuitive way provides the reader who is not familiar with economics the necessary background in order for her to understand the presentation of the material to follow. The most important factors that affect bidding behavior in both simple and multi-unit auctions are also presented. A short discussion on collusion and its impact on auctions are also made.

We begin the presentation of this chapter with an overview of the modern telecoms environment. Recent trends in telecoms driven both by the emerging technologies and the new business models of the telecoms sector are overviewed. Subsequently, a brief overview of the theory and the applications of auctions are provided.

THE TELECOMS MARKET

The impressive growth of the Internet over the past years has resulted in constantly increasing demand for bandwidth. This is evident both at the network edges, where users access the network and at the backbone. The USA Telecom Act of 1996 and similar regulatory interventions throughout the world revolutionized the telecoms market [1]. Large telecom companies dominating the telecommunications market were no longer considered as desired and natural monopolies. Instead, effort was made to bring competition to the market so that more, new, cheaper, more efficient services would be offered to the customers. This was achieved by means of regulatory intervention, which even led to the break ups of the large telecom monopolies, with the most prominent example being the prominent of the AT&T in the United States. This indeed brought fierce competition to the market where multiple providers compete over all the layers of telecoms infrastructure/ connectivity provision as well as services.

Due to the intensifying competition, the network providers of these fixed topology networks now have to provide short-term and customized contracts, whose charge reflects the network load. This is also motivated by the more complex interactions and revenue maximization strategies of the various networks and service providers who may contribute to the provision of a telecom service. The rapidly increasing demand of users for more, better quality and thus more demanding (in terms of resources) services render overprovisioning of resources a policy, which cannot be supported any longer for the entire network infrastructure. No surprise, there has been an increasing interest in new dynamic market-based bandwidth trading mechanisms and more efficient ways of managing and charging the network resources and services. Commercial marketplaces allowing the dynamic reservation by means of auctions of circuits of certain capacity by the interested telecom companies comprise further evidence of this trend [2].

Moreover, the large growth of wireless networks, including the cellular networks, combined with the increasing demand for services, has resulted in increasing demand for the reservation of spectrum; this spectrum is required in order for these networks to provide 2nd (GSM), 2,5 (GPRS) and 3rd (UMTS) generation services. The spectrum of the Radio Access Network is a scarce resource for these networks. At the same time, the 3G services are extremely more demanding than those of 2G networks: Multimedia messages (MMS) replace the short text messages (SMS), while voice calls must still be accommodated along with data (e.g. photo, video, file transfers) services of much higher data rates. The ever-increasing number of mobile devices, the always-on communication paradigm of younger generations also intensified by the explosive growth of social networking and the use of the communication networks and the Internet as the primary infotainment source for myriads of (mobile) users revolutionize the telecoms sector. These facts result in new business opportunities for the telecom carriers but also imply that there is need for both more bandwidth and more importantly for the most efficient usage of the bandwidth that is available.

Finally, the future convergence of the aforementioned technologies with other mobile network technologies and the potential introduction of multicast services also contribute to the dynamic nature of the telecommunications environment. In particular, the trend in the wireless telecom providers is moving towards the "beyond 3G", also referred to as "4G" communication paradigm, where extremely high bit-rate services are offered to the users seamlessly and according to the "Anytime, Anywhere, Always Connected" rationale. The increasing use of wireless technologies to access data services is displayed by a variety of features in the telecoms sector.

In particular, this trend is evident in the computer manufacturing company where new terminals capable of communicating with multiple wireless interfaces (e.g. WLAN and 3G) have already appeared in the market. Also, due to the increasing load of the data services, optical fibers of increasing transport rates are used to interconnect the various wireless antennas/towers. For instance, literally thousands of Verizon Wireless cell sites are interconnected by means of fiber. More details can be found in [3] where it is stated that Verizon intends to invest $5,5 billion towards this direction and from where we quote Quintin Lew, senior vice president of marketing for Verizon Partner Solutions: "In an increasingly wireless-dependent society, cellular carriers like Verizon Wireless are engineering their networks to meet both the exploding voice and data traffic demands of today and the capacity requirements that next-generation wireless technologies like LTE and WiMax will place on their facilities".

Cellular networks but also software giants such as Google by means of its latest Android platform envision a highly dynamic and competitive world where each customer does not belong to the customer base of a provider but rather negotiates, chooses and receives services on-demand. Spectrum markets for wireless operators who can bid for various frequencies and states of ownership have already appeared as well [4]. Thus, there is a new *economy* of wireless infrastructure and services emerging.

The aforementioned discussion suggests that new resource allocation and charging mechanisms are needed in this dynamic context. To this end, *auctions* appear to be the proper trading mechanism. Auctions are very popular in such dynamic economic environments, since they provide a simple, fast and transparent means of determining the price of goods. When properly designed they can also provably maximize the provider's revenue, i.e. attain optimality or the cumulative satisfaction of the users, i.e. maximum social welfare, also referred to as efficiency, is attained.

The adoption of auction mechanisms in this telecoms sector has already made its first steps in the domain of licensing. To be more precise, cellular networks operate by emitting at certain frequency bands, whose ownership belongs to the state. In order for them to allow using the "state spectrum" for making business, they are obliged to obtain a license. These licenses were traditionally allocated by means of time-lengthy hearings that were used to determine which companies would obtain a certain number of licenses; these hearings are referred to in the literature also with the term "beauty contests". This approach was far from efficient (more on this are provided in the remainder of this book) and it was decided that it should be replaced by what became the most prominent and successful example of applying auctions in telecoms: The Simultaneous Multiple Round or Simultaneous Ascending Auction, also commonly referred to as FCC-type auction, which was adopted by the Federal Communications Commission of USA to allocate radio spectrum to wireless service providers.

Therefore, there is an increasing correlation between communication networks and economics, telecoms and auctions. Presenting the various aspects of this interplay, both in the context of business and research for designing more efficient networks and services, is the issue that this book attempts to address and also highlight some of its hopefully interesting aspects.

AUCTIONS

Internet was designed as a technological means of communication suitable for military fault-tolerant networks and subsequently evolved to a means of interconnecting the research and academic institutions. However, since the 90s Internet has become a new means of information sharing and conducting business. Business activity in the Internet is clearly the dominant feature of today's Internet and this trend keeps intensifying. The set of information goods and services offered on top of the Internet are dynamic and evolving towards more user-centric personalized services; the concepts of semantic web, Web 2.0 and the forthcoming Web 3.0 promise a high level of sophistication and personalization which conceptually place the user in the core of the network services and information management. In this dynamic context, price setting of services in such a competitive information economy is nothing but trivial. E-commerce transactions have already exceeded in value those conducted by means of traditional trade and it is envisioned that the use of price bots, auctions and negotiations will soon be the norm. No surprise, there has been a plethora of proposals regarding systems, architectures and agents who comprise various parts of the new information economy.

An extremely popular means of trade in this dynamic new economy, which is based on the notion of competition, is that of *auctions*. Auction is a market mechanism which relies on the submission of bids by its customers, who are typically referred to as *bidders*; alternatively, the term *players* is also used in the context of game-theoretic analysis of auctions.

Auctions are a special form of a *game*, and fully described by a set of rules. The term game is used to denote a well-defined means of strategic interaction among rational entities, each having and pursuing different and most likely conflicting interests and goals respectively. The specification of the game rules unambiguously specify the possible *actions* of the market participants, i.e. who can do what, what is and is not allowed, and when.

These "game" rules apply to the auctions as well and they are also complemented in the auctions context by the *winner determination rule* and the *payment rule*. As its name indicates, the *winner determination rule* prescribes who is (or are) declared as winner(s) in the auction and based on what criteria. This rule is complemented by the *payment rule*, which defines the charge of the auction winner(s). It is imperative that the auction rules are *binding*, i.e. once announced cannot be subsequently modified or cancelled, even by the entity conducting the auction, i.e. the *auctioneer*. Even the rules for the potential cancellation of an auction must be explicitly defined and announced *a priori*, i.e. before the actual auction takes place.

Auctions typically comprise of two phases: the bid submission phase and the winner determination phase. The former is the part of the auction where bidders place their bids. The start of this phase is common knowledge, i.e. known to all the auction participants. The time length of this phase may be preannounced or decided a posteriori, based on rules and the activity observed in the auction. The winner determination phase follows the bid submission phase and comprises of computing the auction winners, i.e. deciding which users are allocated what.

Commercial sites that host user-initiated auctions, such as *Ebay* [5] perform transactions of many millions of dollars on a daily basis. The creation of more sophisticated services and information products, such as auction *newsletters*, *software* and *bidding agents*, *specialized search engines* and *bulletin boards* comprise additional evidence of the increasing interest of the public for auctions.

Auctions have been used extensively throughout all phases of human history. Interestingly, the term auction is derived from the (both ancient and modern) Greek word "ΑΥΞΟΝ" and its subsequent Latin (Roman) transcript "AUCTION". Though the meaning of both these ancient words is ascending, there are auction mechanisms where the auction price does not necessarily increase. Description of auctions can be found in a plethora of both poetic and historic texts, such as the ancient Greek history of Herodotus [6].

The on-going popular and continuous use of auctions in human society is no surprising. Auctions comprise a fast, simple, transparent and efficient means of determining the market value of goods and services.

Designing auction mechanism involves game-theoretic incentives analysis so that the auction can achieve *revenue maximization* and/or *social welfare maximization*. *Revenue maximization*, also denoted with the term *optimality*, is attained if the seller's revenues are maximized by means of the auction outcome. *Social welfare maximization*, also referred to as *efficiency*, implies that the auctioned item(s) are awarded to the user(s) that need/value them the most. More formally, the sum of all the economy's agents' utilities is maximized; a detailed definition of utility functions is provided in the remainder of this chapter.

All these features make auctions an ideal means of trade for goods whose value is either undetermined by their owner or varies a lot over time. A typical example of such a setting are the wholesale flower and tulips auctions taking place in the Netherlands [7], where traders from all over the world can physically and electronically purchase large quantities of tulips and other flowers grouped in *lots*.

Clearly, using fixed prices in this setting would be far from efficient, optimal or desirable, due to the fluctuations of demand and supply but also most importantly due to the variance in the quality of the flowers of the various lots. Other contexts where auctions are typically used are markets of fresh fish, vegetables and flowers, diamonds, crude oil, electricity, security and treasury bonds for financing national debt [8], [9].

In the remainder of this book we focus on the telecoms sector and describe how auctions have been applied and for what goods and services. We also present some academic research approaches that propose and argue on the merits of the use of auctions for resource allocation in the telecom networks of today and the near future.

We now proceed to present some fundamental economics and auction theory concepts and terms that are required for the reader to follow the presentation of the topics covered in the remainder of this book.

FUNDAMENTAL ECONOMICS AND AUCTION THEORY CONCEPTS

We begin the presentation of this section with an overview of some fundamental terms and results of the economic theory. The material presented in this chapter, as well as additional details, can be founded by the interested reader in [8], [9], [10], and [11].

Utility Function

The utility function is one of the fundamental mathematical tools of the economic theory. It is used in a variety of economic models in order to provide quantification, i.e. a measure of the satisfaction which results for a consumer from being allocated either a set of goods or a quantity of units of a good. Note that in order for a participant of an auction (i.e. a bidder) to be able to take part in an auction, it is imperative that she has expressed her relative preferences for all the possible outcomes of the auction. Therefore, the auction theory also makes use of the notion of the *utility function*; this is needed since the utility function reflects and quantifies the aforementioned preferences of the user.

We now proceed to provide a more formal definition of the utility function: A function $u: \Omega \to R$ is defined as a utility function if it orders and quantifies the preferences of the bidder. That is, it maps every possible outcome of the auction from the sampling Ω to a real number. For instance, the following functions, namely $u_1(\cdot)$ and $u_2(\cdot)$, are valid utility functions for a bidder who values the auction outcome α as twice better than β, with the latter being equivalent for her to the outcome γ; Both outcomes β and γ are strictly more preferable than δ, with the latter being a not desirable outcome for the bidder:

$u_1(\alpha) = 1$, $u_1(\beta) = 1/2$, $u_1(\gamma) = 1/2$ and $u_1(\delta) = 0$

$u_2(\alpha) = 500$, $u_2(\beta) = 250$, $u_2(\gamma) = 250$ and $u_2(\delta) = 0$

This presentation of the utility functions $u_1(\cdot)$ and $u_2(\cdot)$ displays the fundamental property of a utility function: A utility function provides an ordering of the preferences of the various possible outcomes of a game for a player. This basic property simplifies the decision-making process of the player and more importantly provides a mathematical abstraction of the auction or more generally a game. To be more specific, in order for the player to find the outcome ω of the game, which is the most preferable for the player, it suffices to compute the outcome ω, which maximizes the player's utility function. Therefore, it is equivalent for the player to solve the problem $u(\omega) = \max_{s \in S} u(s)$.

The utility function $u(q)$ can also be used to quantify the utility that results for a player from obtaining a quantity q of a good, e.g. units of bandwidth, by means of an auction. However, the definition of such a utility function, as also depicted by the aforementioned presentation of the utility functions $u_1(\cdot)$ and $u_2(\cdot)$, is not unique. A useful and common simplification that is used to overcome this "problem", which holds also for the remainder of this book, is that the utility function expresses the amount of money that a consumer would pay (i.e. the willingness to pay) in order to obtain a certain quantity/combination of goods. This coupling of the utility function definition with the user's actual willingness to pay eliminates the issue of multiple utility functions per user, and allows us to assume that each user's preferences can be accurately expressed by a unique utility function.

For instance, in the case of a telecom provider who is interested in leasing bandwidth in order to be able to accommodate the traffic of its subscribers, there is a unique utility function that expresses how much each provider and each user values the various quantities of bandwidth. This also implies that the maximum amount of money that each user is willing to pay for the various quantities of bandwidth is also defined.

The *marginal utility* is defined as the additional utility attained from one additional unit of a good or, more formally, the derivative of utility with respect to the quantity of this good. The marginal utility is an important concept because agents consider marginal utilities when deciding how much to purchase and consume.

There are various forms of utility functions. Depending on the form of the utility function, users (and services) can be classified to the following categories:

- *Guaranteed:* This type of users' demand consists of a single point. Thus, these users are only satisfied by being allocated a certain quantity of a good.
- *Elastic:* These users obtain in general different utility from being allocated different quantities of a good. The typical case for this type of utility function is that the utility obtained from an additional unit (i.e. the *marginal utility*) decreases with the quantity of units. This case is also referred to in the literature as the case of *diminishing returns*.

Demand Function

We have already defined the notion of utility function as the function that provides a mapping of any given amount of a good (or alternatively combination of discrete goods) to the user's willingness to pay. Assuming the typical assumption of the auction theory literature that the utility function is continuous and differentiable, we can obtain the inverse function of the utility functions. This is defined as the demand function.

By construction, the demand function is the function, which provides a mapping of any given amount of money to a certain quantity of good that the user is willing to buy. Obviously, if any of the two functions, namely either the utility function or the demand function are given, one can easily derive the other.

Without loss of generality and in order to facilitate the presentation it is henceforth assumed in the remainder of this book, unless if explicitly stated otherwise, that utility/demand functions pertain to the quantity of bandwidth being allocated to/demanded by users of communication networks.

Net Benefit

In order for a consumer to purchase a quantity q of a good, she must obviously take into account not only the utility she obtains from being allocated the q units of the good, which is denoted as $u(q)$, but also the amount of money she would have to pay in order to purchase those units. Hence, the charge that the user has to incur, denoted as $c(q)$, must be also taken into account.

Obviously, it is only meaningful for a consumer to purchase a certain quantity of goods only as long as the utility obtained from the allocation of the goods exceeds the cost incurred. The difference of the utility obtained from the outcome of a game (e.g. the allocation of q units of a good) minus the respective charge incurred is defined as *net benefit NB(q) = u(q) – c(q)*.

TYPES OF UTILITY FUNCTIONS

In this subsection we present the most common forms of utility functions that are used to describe the utility that users of communication networks obtain from being awarded a certain quantity of bandwidth along with a service.

Based on the user's selection of one of these utility functions, we obtain the following classification of communication networks users.

Guaranteed

This is the type of users that are satisfied only if they are allocated just one given quantity of bandwidth. To be more precise, for this kind of users:

- A certain quantity of bandwidth is of a certain positive value.
- Any quantity of bandwidth, which is less than the one desired is useless, i.e. the utility obtained from it is considered to be zero.
- Any quantity of bandwidth, which is more than the one desired does not result in any additional utility compared to the one obtained from the allocation of the desired quantity of bandwidth. It is worth noting that since any additional quantity of bandwidth is of zero value, the allocation of such a higher quantity of bandwidth is actually in the expense of the user. This is due to the fact that the user will have to incur an additional monetary cost for paying for the extra units of bandwidth that are of zero value to her, thus deteriorating her own *net benefit*.

The form of the utility function for this kind of users is depicted as Figure 1.1. This step-like type of utility function is very common in cellular communication networks and is applicable to users demanding services such as video streaming, where the video has been precoded at a given quality, i.e. bit-rate.

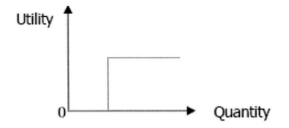

Figure 1.1. The utility function of a user who is of the guaranteed type.

A variation of this utility function is the sigmoid utility function, where a steep S-like line replaces the two 90 degrees angles and vertical line of the step utility function. This variation provides a higher degree of tolerance to the utility (e.g. a network application) for quantities close to that determined by the step utility function. This is also meaningful in telecommunication services where e.g. for a streaming application there might be a small tolerance to rate fluctuations due to the fact that user terminals are typically equipped with a playout buffer.

Elastic

This type of users obtains positive utility by being allocated a plethora of quantities of bandwidth. It is typical for this type of utility functions in the context of concave networks to be concave. This means that the user utility function is continuous and twice differentiable; also the additional (i.e. marginal) value that users obtain from the allocation of an additional unit of bandwidth is diminishing over quantity. Thus, for elastic users each additional acquired unit is of less value to them compared to that attained by the previous unit. A typical form of an elastic user's concave utility function is depicted as Figure 1.2.

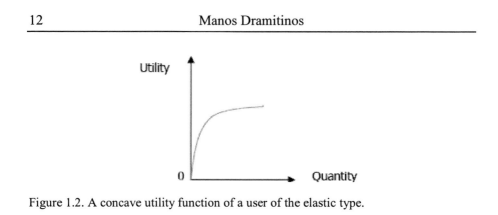

Figure 1.2. A concave utility function of a user of the elastic type.

Note that another interesting type of utility function of this category of users is the linear utility function where the allocation of all units of bandwidth is of the same value to the user compared to the allocation of any other previous unit.

Elastic with Minimum Guarantees

This type of users is a hybrid of the two aforementioned categories. It pertains to users that demand the allocation of a minimum quantity of resources so that they can obtain a positive utility. This characteristic is similar to what users of the guaranteed type pursue. However, as opposed to users of the guaranteed type, the allocation of additional units of bandwidth results in additional positive utility for the user. A typical form of this kind of utility function is depicted as Figure 1.3.

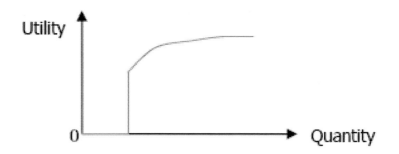

Figure 1.3. The utility function of a user with minimum guarantees.

CLASSIFICATION OF AUCTIONS

There are multiple ways to classify the various auction mechanisms. Some of the most commonly used classifications are provided below. An auction is referred to as being:

- *Simple (single-unit)* when just one item is to be auctioned.
- *Multi-object* when multiple items are to be auctioned. The auctions of this category can be further classified as:

  o *Homogeneous*, provided that the auctioned items are identical, i.e. all objects are of the same type. The homogeneous multi-object auctions where all the auctioned items are units of a divisible good, e.g. units of bandwidth of a link, are typically referred to as *multi-unit* auctions.

  o *Heterogeneous*, provided that the auctioned items are not similar, i.e. the objects are of multiple items. For instance, in the context of telecoms this is the case when multiple chunks of different frequencies and quantity of wireless spectrum are auctioned to telecom companies.

  o *Combinatorial*, if the auction rules allow the submission of bids for combinations of the auctioned items, i.e. allow combinatorial bids. This is the case for example, is for an auction for two items, namely A and B, the bidders are allowed to place one bid for the combination of A and B. This is a useful feature when there are *complementarities* among the auctioned items and thus the acquisition of two objects may bring to the bidder higher value than the sum of valuations of the bidder for A and B. (This property of the respective bidder's utility function is commonly referred to as *super-additive* in the literature.) A typical example where such complementarities exist is at land auctions: Clearly, the allocation of two neighboring pieces of land results in higher value for the owner as opposed to the case where those pieces of land were far apart and is higher than the user's valuation for the first piece of land plus his respective valuation for the second piece of land.

o   *Independent*, if combinatorial bids are prohibited and an individual's multiple bids for some of the auctioned items that are of his interest are treated independently by the auctioneer.

Both simple and multi-object auctions can be further classified as:

- *Open*, assuming that the bidding process prescribes that bids are either made in public by the bidders or equivalently the auctioneer publicly announces them.
- *Sealed-bid*, in case the bids are submitted in the form of sealed tenders. Note that in this case each bidder cannot observe the bids of his competitors, as opposed to open auctions.

The price path of the auction is also of importance. Based on this criterion, we can obtain the following classification of auctions:

- *Ascending-price* auctions are the auctions where the auction price is initially low (or even zero) and is subsequently gradually incremented as the auction proceeds, either by the auctioneer or the users' bids.
- *Descending-price* (or *Dutch*) auctions are the auctions where the auction price is initially set to a high value and is gradually decremented as the auction proceeds.

The aforementioned classification is based on the number and type of the auctioned items, as well as the type of bids allowed in the multi-object case. However, there are several other criteria that also can provide a further classification of the various auction mechanisms. For instance, multi-object auctions can be further classified according to the time of auctioning of the multiple items.

Thus, multi-object auctions can be further distinguished as:

- *Simultaneous*, if all the items are auctioned at the same time.
- *Sequential*, in case the items are auctioned one after another, i.e. each item is auctioned separately. Under sequential auctioning, the auctioneer will initially auction the first item. Once this auction has finished and the first item has been awarded to the standing bidder, he proceeds to auction the next item, and so on.

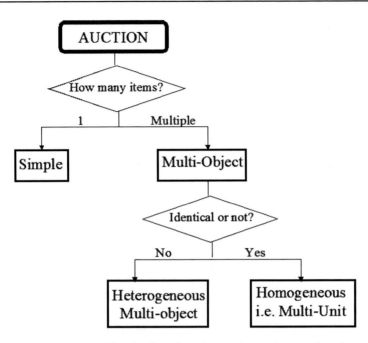

Figure 1.4. An auction classification based on the number and type of goods auctioned.

Moreover, based on the auction's payment rule, an auction mechanism can be classified as:

- *Standard*, if the winner(s) of the auctioned item(s) is (are) the only bidder(s) who has (have) to pay a certain amount of money to the auctioneer, while the bidders who did not win anything at the auction are not charged[1]. Typically, both theory and practice of auctions focus on the standard auction mechanisms.
- *Non-standard*, in case the rules of the standard auction do not apply. The most well-known example of non-standard auction used in the literature is that of an all-pay auction for an item: Under this auction format all users bid in order to be awarded an item and the auction rules prescribe that all of them will have to pay their bids, regardless of the fact that only the highest bidder will be awarded the auctioned item.

---

[1] This classification refers to the actual allocation and payment rule of the auction and not to the presence or not of entry fees for the auction.

Finally, once more based on the payment rule, the multi-unit auctions can be classified to:

- *Uniform–price* auctions, when there is a common price, which is paid by all bidders for the units awarded.
- *Discriminatory* auctions, if the payment rule prescribes that the various winners pay in general different amounts of money. The simplest and best-known example of such an auction mechanism payment rule is the pay-your-bid, which prescribes that each user pays his winning bids.

It is worth noting that so far and for all the aforementioned auction mechanism classifications we have implicitly assumed that only the bidders submit bids. It is also possible for a multi-object auction to prescribe that bidders will submit bids in order to express demand for resources, while sellers will place requests for price (formally called *asks*) for the resources owned and auctioned. This way both the demand and the supply function for the goods auctioned are dynamically constructed through the bidding process. Such auctions are called *double auctions* and will also be presented in detail in the remainder of this book.

Finally, another possibility for the seller in a multi-unit auction is not to award to the bidders the total quantity of units of the good auctioned, provided that the auction rules allow this. This kind of auctions is called *auctions of variable quantity* and under these auction schemes the seller typically decided on the quantity of units to be sold after he collects the users' bids. He then decides on the quantity to be sold based on the optimization of a certain criterion, which typically is his revenue.

FACTORS AFFECTING BIDDING BEHAVIOR

In this section, we present the main factors, which along with the user utility functions and the auction rules greatly affect the behavior of the bidders throughout the auction, i.e. determine their *bidding strategy*. The interested reader may acquire additional information on this issue from [8], [9], [10], [11], [12], [13] that present in detail most of the material of this section. In order to facilitate the presentation and without loss of generality in the remainder of this section we mostly discuss the factors that affect users' bidding behavior in the context of simple auctions. However, the applicability of the presentation is more general and thus can be straightforwardly applied to all kinds of auction mechanisms.

Information Model

An issue of great importance for the bidders and their corresponding bidding strategy is obviously how they determine the actual value that they will obtain from the acquisition of the auctioned item, i.e. how much the item is actually worth to them. In general, a bidder's value may just depend on his private information but it can also be the case that the user's valuation is affected from information about the valuations of the rival bidders. Therefore, we can say that each user's both valuation and bid heavily depend on the *information model* of the auction.

We now proceed to present a classification of the various auction information models.

Independent Private Values

In this case, each bidder is certain about how much he values the auctioned item. This value is obtained solely by his utility function and is completely independent to the valuations of the other bidders competing in the auction.

A typical assumption in the literature, which is useful for the analysis of the various auction mechanisms, is that these *independent private values* (or *i.p.v.* for short) are also drawn from some random distribution. Therefore, this assumption pertains to the case where each bidder's i respective valuation v_i is actually a random variable drawn from a distribution with a cumulative probability function F_i. A further simplification of the independent previous values case, which is very useful since it facilitates greatly the analysis of the auction and the derivation of the user bidding strategies, is that all user valuations are (once more independently) drawn from the same distribution; this simply means that the distribution from which the bidders valuations are drawn is the same for all users. The term *independent identically distributed* values (or *i.i.d* for short) is used to refer to the case. Due to the fact that the latter case implies symmetry on bidders' valuations, the corresponding information model is commonly referred to as *symmetric independent private values* model (or *S.I.P.V.* for short).

This model is used for the majority of auction theory research works and is mostly applicable for cases where the auctioned item's inherent characteristics are perceived as being of different value by the bidders, based on their respective heterogeneous preferences. A typical example is bidding for an item, e.g. a piece of art, which will be simply "used" by its future owner and not be resold.

Obviously, under the *independent private values* information model a bidder will not modify either his valuation or his bid in the auction in case a rival's valuation for the auctioned item is revealed to him.

Common Value

The *common value* information model is the opposite extreme of the private values model. The *common value* information model prescribes that the auctioned item is actually of exactly the same value to all the bidders. However, each user has different information, i.e. different estimation, on the exact value of the auctioned item. The object's real value can be accurately estimated upon its acquisition and will be the same for all the competing bidders, regardless of who actually won the auction.

Under this model, the bidders try to estimate this common value of the good auctioned. In particular, bidder's i valuation v_i can be described as being $v_i = v + \varepsilon_i$, where v pertains to the common value of the good, while ε_i is the "noise" of bidder's estimate.

A typical example where this model can be straightforwardly applied is that of auctioning a jar of coins or oil drilling licenses. In both cases, the value of the item is the same to all bidders and depends only on the quantity of coins or oil respectively that is to be actually allocated. However, the bidders can only find out the exact value of this unknown quantity after the auction has ended (*ex post*). The noise of estimate is the deviation of the user's "guessing" from this actual quantity.

Affiliated Values

The *affiliated values* information model can be seen as a hybrid model of both the independent private values model and the common value model. It is used to describe a situation where each bidder's valuation depends on and is affected by how highly his competitors value the item as well.

A typical example is the auction of a piece of art among art dealers who aim to resell it to their clients. It is clear that each bidder has a certain "private value" which pertains to how highly each person values that piece of art. In addition to that, there is also a guessing of how much the market would be willing to pay for it, i.e. what its resale value would be.

It should be clear to the reader that each individual's valuation would be modified and biased on the rival bidders' valuation if such information were available.

Risk Aversion

Risk aversion is a term used to denote the sensitivity of a user towards the danger of losing the auctioned item. It depicts the impact of uncertainty over the final outcome of a game to the bidder's utility and bidding behavior.

- A bidder who is not affected by this uncertainty and simply attempts to maximize his expected payoff from a game or auction is referred to as *risk neutral*.
- On the contrary, if the uncertainty has impact on the user's utility, thus reducing the value of payoffs of uncertain outcomes, this type of bidders is referred to as being *risk averse*. In auctions, this category of bidders try to mitigate the risk of losing by placing higher (in terms of willingness to pay) bids in an auction, compared to those that would have been submitted if the bidder were risk neutral.

In the literature, the various degrees of "sensitivity" of users towards the risk of losing in the auction can be formulated by means of proper utility functions definitions. This sensitivity and corresponding utility function definition clearly affects the bids that are to be submitted by the bidder in the auction. In particular, let as assume that a bidder interested in reserving units of bandwidth participates in an auction. Let as denote with x a quantity of bandwidth and with $c(x)$ the corresponding user's charge for reserving this quantity of bandwidth. It can be formulated that the user's risk aversion remains constant with respect to the quantity of units allocated (Constant Absolute Risk Aversion) or varies (Constant Relative Risk Aversion) according to a sensitivity parameter α. The respective utility function definitions are as follows:

$$u(x,c) := -1/a \cdot e^{-ax} - c(x), \qquad a > 0 \ (\text{CARA})$$

$$u(x,c) := -1/(1-a) \cdot x^{1-a} - c(x), \qquad a \in (0,1] \, (\text{CRRA})$$

In general, it is the case that the higher the risk aversion of a bidder is, then the more aggressive he bids in the auction. Extreme risk aversion results in essentially asymptotically truthful bids, even for first-price auctions.

Budget Constraints – Entry Fees

Another factor greatly affecting users' bidding behavior is the existence or absence respectively of either *budget constraints* or *entry fees*.

The term *budget constraints* is used to denote the fact that despite the fact that a bidder may value the auctioned item very highly, he cannot actually pay that amount of money that is equal to his valuation because his budget is lower. Budget constraints are actually common in the telecoms context where companies bidding for spectrum licenses must have acquired sufficient creditability, by means of bank guarantees that are given to the auctioneer (the state), in order to bid a certain amount of money. In most telecom auctions companies were forced to redraw from pursuing a spectrum license due to budget constraints.

Entry fees pertain to the case where all bidders admitted to an auction are forced to pay a certain amount of money to the auctioneer. The auctioneer uses the presence of entry fees in order to make sure that only serious and determined bidders will take place in the auction. This is crucial also in the case of telecom auctions, in order to assure that telecom resources are awarded to companies who are seriously determined to deploy new services and in order to mitigate the logistics and complexity of actually running the auction. However, the introduction of entry fees in the auction by the auctioneer may deter entry, i.e. participation, of companies who believe that are not as strong as their competitors and thus have slim chances of winning anything in the auction. This way, competition can be mitigated, affecting the remaining bidders' strategies and the corresponding values of the auction revenue and the social welfare attained.

Experience and Winner's Curse in Common Value Auctions

The preparation and the experience of the bidder is always another crucial factor that affects their bidding behavior and thus the auction outcome. In particular, in the common value information model it has been observed that users of limited experience often fail to update their respective valuations in a rational way. Instead, under ascending auction formats, they tend to be carried out by the auction and end up overbidding for the auctioned item. Thus, they often claim it for a bid that is higher than its respective valuation.

The latter phenomenon implies that bidders are not acting perfectly rationally. Therefore, such behavior cannot be in general captured by the auction formulations of the literature, where individuals are taken to be perfectly rational. This difference of theory and practice is not considered to be significant, since in important auctions involving the selling of items of high value, either all users act rationally or those who act irrationally are typically low-value bidders who are dropped out of the auction very early, thus not affecting its outcome in terms of either the final allocations of the auctioned item(s) or the payments.

Note also that this irrational bidding behavior intensifies the *winner's curse*. This term is used to denote the fact that the person who was awarded the item has by definition overbidded its value. It is also worth emphasizing that the winner's curse may appear even if all users are perfectly rational and in particular under the common value information model: Since the item awarded is of the same value to all the auction participants, then by definition it is awarded to the person who bidded the most, i.e. overestimated it the most. The latter is taken into account by rational bidders who bias their bids on the event of overestimating the item's value. In fact, the less information is revealed in the auction and thus the less clear how the bid should be biased, the more afraid the bidders are of the winner's curse, thus further lowering their bids. A detailed presentation of these issues is beyond the scope of this book. The reader may refer to [11], [12] and [14] for more on this.

Finally, it is worth noting that winner's curse has been documented even in certain dramatic events in history, even from the ancient times. For instance, in 193 A.D., after the death of Caesar Pertinax, the Praetorian Guard actually auctioned the entire Roman Empire to the ambitious Roman nobles. Note that the common value information model is well fitted to the auction, since the value of the empire is actually its wealth, which can be accumulated by the emperor mostly by means of taxation of his subjects. Estimating however this exact amount of money, that is how much the Roman Empire is really worth, is a quite difficult task, especially if performed in ancient times with lack of any detailed information and sophisticated models. The auction was finally won by Marcus Didius Salvius Julianus, who overbidded his rivals. However, the newly proclaimed Caesar did not manage to collect the promised amount of money in order to fulfill his promises to the Praetorian Guard. No surprise, he was murdered by the Praetorians soon after his enthronement. Clearly, this is likely to be among the most extreme and unfortunate cases of winner's curse in history [15].

CONCLUSION

Collusion is a phenomenon where a set (formally called *ring)* of bidders agrees to create an "alliance" and to behave in the auction as a coalition with all its members serving the coalition's aim. This strategy aims at reducing the competition in the auction by cooperating instead of competing, since the collusion members don't compete against each other trying to satisfy their individual goals. Hence, in practice it is just one of the ring's members that is bidding aggressively in the auction, while the other members submit very low bids that have no chance of winning. This way competition is reduced and it is possible for the ring (and in particular the ring member having the highest value for the item) to acquire it for a very low price. Obviously collusion is a highly undesirable strategy for the auctioneer, and also often punishable by law, due to the reduction of his corresponding revenue.

The typical collusion scenario is that multiple players form rings. Tha aim of those rings is the acquisition of the auctioned item for the lowest possible price. In order for the ring members to decide who will be the ring's standing bidder in the auction, they typically perform a pre-auction of the item with the ring members being the bidders. The bids at this pre-auction are binding for the ring members, in the sense that they are used to define who will be the ring member actually competing in the real auction; obviously this is the standing bidder of this collusion ring pre-auction of the item. Once the ring has acquired the auctioned item, the winner performs *side-payments* to the other ring members. The exact value of these side-payments is computed based on the ring members' valuations, which were revealed at the pre-auction and are such that all the ring members are better off with colluding than if they were bidding honestly in the auction.

An alternative form of collusion can occur in auctions that are frequently repeated and where the same, typically small set of bidders is competing against each other all the time. In this context, it is possible for the bidders to collude so that they all win some of the auctions conducted. Once again, the number of the auctions where each member of the ring will be the standing bidder depends on the bidders' valuations and budget constraints. This way, it is attempted by the ring members to totally manipulate the auction and avoid any actual competitive bidding and corresponding high charges at any of the auctions. It is clear that once again the auctioneer's revenues are mitigated by the collusion of the bidders.

A notable example of such a collusion scheme is the auction conducted by the U.S. National Treasury in order to finance public debt. Finally, it should be noted that depending on the auction's rules, it may be possible or not for the bidders to collude. The following chapters contain more material on the susceptibility of the various auction mechanisms to collusion.

In this chapter we briefly presented some fundamental concepts and terms form both economics and auction theory. We have presented a way to perform a detailed classification of the plethora of auction mechanisms of the literature. This is important for the study of auctions, since the pros and cons of each class of mechanisms that pertain to each part of this classification are used in auction mechanism design to justify the selection of a certain class of mechanisms over the alternative designs. We further elaborate on this issue on the remainder of this book where certain case studies of auction mechanism design shall be presented. The most important factors that affect bidding behavior in both simple and multi-unit auctions have also been presented. Finally, the issues of winner's curse and collusion have been also addressed and their impact on the bidders' strategies has been documented.

REFERENCES

[1]   Economides, N. Telecommunications Regulation: An Introduction, *Working Paper EC-03-22*, Stern School of Business, NY, September 2003, revised August 2004.

[2]   Bandwidth Market Ltd., http://www.bandwidthmarket.com/.

[3]   Lightwave article, Verizon opens up fiber-optic network to wireless carriers, http://lw.pennnet.com/Articles/Article_Display.cfm?Section= ARTCLandSubSection=DisplayandPUBLICATION_ID=13andARTIC LE_ID=357525andcmpid=EnlDirectMarch272009.

[4]   SpecEx, http://www.specex.com/index/.

[5]   Ebay, http://www.ebay.com/.

[6]   Herodotus, The Histories, 5th century BC.

[7]   Van Heck, E.; Ribbers, P. Experiences with Electronic Auctions in the Dutch Flower Industry, *Global Electronic Commerce: Theory and Case Studies*, 355—366, The MIT Press, Cambridge, MA, 1999.

[8] Courcoubetis, C.; Weber R. *Pricing Communication Networks: Economics, Technology and Modelling*, John Wiley and Sons, 2003, ISBN 0-4708-5130-9.

[9] Binmore, K. *Fun and Games: A Text on Game Theory*, Houghton Mifflin, 1991, ISBN 0-6692-4603-4.

[10] Klemperer, P. Auction Theory: A Guide to the Literature, *Journal of Economic Surveys*, 13:3, 1999.

[11] Krishna, V. *Auction Theory*, Academic Press, April 2002, ISBN 0-1242-6297-X.

[12] McAfee, P.; McMillan, J. Auctions and Bidding, *Journal of Economic Literature*, 25:2, 699-738, 1987.

[13] Wolfstetter, E. *Topics in Microeconomics*, Cambridge University Press, 1999.

[14] Cramton, P.; Kerr S. Tradable Carbon Permit Auctions: How and Why to Auction Not Grandfather, *Energy Policy*, 30, 333-345, 2002.

[15] Columbia Encyclopedia, URL: http://www.encyclopedia.com/doc/1E1-DidiusJu.html

Chapter 2

SIMPLE AUCTIONS

ABSTRACT

This chapter focuses on the presentation of the most popular and best-known simple (i.e. single-unit) auction mechanisms. There is extensive literature about the simple auction mechanisms, their analysis and properties. The material presented in this chapter, as well as additional details, can be founded by the interested reader in [1], [2], [3], [4], [5] and [6]. Though simple auctions regard the sale of just a single item, the basic simple auction formats presented in this chapter can be generalized for the sale of multiple items or units of a homogeneous good. The latter family of auction mechanisms is presented in the next chapter of this book.

INTRODUCTION

Simple (also referred to as single-unit) auctions pertain to the case where a single item is auctioned. As understood by the self-explanatory name of this type of auctions, this is actually the simplest kind of auctions in terms of both ease of comprehension and analysis and derivation of the users' bidding strategies. However, the simplicity of these auctions does not mitigate these auctions' usefulness or popularity. In particular, some of the best-known auction mechanisms, which are widely used nowadays, are actually simple auctions. Companies like eBay also gain significant amounts of money by hosting simple auctions. This chapter contains a presentation of the most important and most widely used simple auction formats, as well as some fundamental auction theory results thereof.

THE ENGLISH AUCTION

Presentation

This is probably the best-known auction and what most people think first when the term "auction" is brought up. The English auction rules prescribe that the physical presence of all bidders is required[2].

The seller initially starts by asking from the bidders to bid the minimum acceptable price for which the item auctioned may be sold, i.e. he demands the *reserve price*. The reserve price may be either a positive amount of money or zero. The price of the auction is subsequently gradually increased and this monotonic process is repeated until there is only one bidder willing to match the price demanded by the auctioneer. Then, the item is awarded to the highest bidder.

There are several possible formats of this auction based on whether the auction is physically conducted or by means of specialized software. Also another important aspect of the auction is how bidders' bids are conveyed to the auctioneer. The most commonly used signaling systems for this type of auction comprise:

- Open outcry of the bid by the auctioneer and hand signaling of the bidders if they are willing to bid the demanded amount of money,
- The bidders raising the price of the auction by submitting open outcry bids to the auctioneer who simply repeats them to the room asking for this bid to be topped.
- The auction price is announced by the auctioneer or displayed onto an electronic screen and bidders keep pressing a button for as long as they are willing to claim the auctioned item for the given price. Once they release the button, they essentially quit the auction. This version of the English auction is also referred to in the literature as *ascending clock* auction.

---

[2] This is actually an over simplification since it is possible for bidders to participate in English auctions remotely via phone and by means of physical or electronic software agents who act on their behalf.

Bidding Strategies

It is easy to observe that it is best for the bidder of an English auction to gradually increase his bid with the minimum bid increment, as long as the auction price is less than or equal to his valuation for the auctioned item. Once the auction price exceeds his respective valuation, it is best for her to withdraw from the auction. This way, he can always be sure that the probability of winning the item is maximized and that she always attains positive net benefit, i.e. some profit. The limit case of this strategy is the case where the bidder is awarded the item for a price equal to her respective valuation; in this case the attained net benefit is zero. Also note that the adoption of this strategy implies that the auction winner simply outbids the bidder with the second highest valuation in the bidding population. Therefore, the expected payment of the winner equals the second highest valuation of the bidders.

Under either the common value or the affiliated values information model, it has been observed in practice that the ascending format of the auction results in overbidding by inexperienced and enthusiastic bidders. However, when all users are bidding rationally, the ascending format actually can help them protect themselves against winner's curse. This is due to the fact that the entire market demand for the auctioned item is observed. Therefore, the information revealed in the auction process can help the bidders to dynamically update by means of performing a Bayesian update of their respective valuation for the object. This promotes competition since aggressive bidding is not mitigated by the fear of the winner's curse, as opposed to a sealed-bid auction where no information regarding the market value of the object auctioned is revealed.

Properties

Overall the English auction reveals much information regarding how highly the various bidders actually value the item auctioned. This is obviously due to the open and ascending price format of the auction. In particular, the complete aggregate demand function of the bidders for the auctioned item is revealed, since the drop out points of all the competing bidders are publicly observable.

This also promotes aggressive bidding in the common value and affiliated values information model since the fear of winner's curse is mitigated. Moreover, this auction mechanism is the most susceptible to collusion. This is extremely important since collusion results in mitigation of the competition and a corresponding reduction of the seller's revenue.

In particular, under the English (open) auction format, collusion is self-enforcing for the ring members. Since all bidders can observe the bids of their rivals, it is impossible for any collusion ring member to deviate and place a high bid in the auction because such an action will be immediately observed by the other members of the ring; in this case the standing bidder of the ring will simply outbid the deviating member, which will also not receive any side payment due to its deviation. Thus, it is dominant strategy for a ring member to remain loyal to the collusion ring.

THE FIRST-PRICE SEALED-BID AUCTION

Presentation

As indicated by this auction's name, bids are submitted in the form of sealed tenders to the auctioneer up to a publicly announced deadline. This way, each bidder is only aware of her own bid. Upon the expiration of the bid submission deadline, the auctioneer opens the collected bids and sorts them with respect to the price.

The bidder who submitted the highest bid is the auction's winner and is allocated the auctioned item. The charge of the winner is equal to his bid. There are variations of this mechanism under which either only the highest bid is publicly announced or alternative all the collected bids.

Bidding Strategies

Placing a high bid has two conflicting properties: First of all, it increases the probability of the bid to top the rival bids and thus to be declared as the winning bid in the auction. However, on the same time, since each bidder has to pay his bid, it reduces the bidder's surplus, his net benefit from winning the auctioned item. Indeed, it is easy to see that if the bid is truthful, that is equal to the bidder's valuation for the auctioned item, and then the winner of the auction attains literally zero net benefit. A meaningful strategy for this type of auction is to submit a bid, which is lower than the actual user's valuation, i.e. perform *bid shading*.

This optimal bid shading, i.e. the exact amount by which the bid would lower than the respective bidder's valuation can be sometimes computed under some standard model assumptions: In particular, let us assume that all the auction participants are risk neutral. Furthermore, and without loss of generality, let us assume that users' valuations are independently drawn from a uniform distribution having support in *[0, 1]*. Each bidder is obviously aware of his valuation and does not disclose this information to his rivals.

Moreover, the way valuations are drawn, i.e. the uniform distribution and its support, are assumed to be *common knowledge*: This means that all bidders are aware of these facts and are also aware that their rivals are also aware of the distribution and its support as well.

Furthermore, let us assume that all the bidders also know the number of competing bidders in the auction m. Under these assumptions, it is proven that the optimal amount of bid shading for the bidders is $\dfrac{1}{m}$. This means that given that a user's valuation for the auctioned item is u, then it is optimal to place a bid equal to $u \cdot \left(1 - \dfrac{1}{m}\right)$. This is proven to be the amount of bid shading that maximized the bidder's expected gain from the auction, i.e. the expectation of the probability of winning times the net benefit attained.

The aforementioned optimal bid shading result is quite general for simple auctions. This is the optimal bid shading to be performed both for the first-price sealed-bid auction and the Dutch auction, which is presented in the remainder of this chapter.

Properties

It is easy to see that under the symmetric bidders model presented in the previous subsection, the auction is efficient, i.e. maximizes social welfare. Since all users shade their bids by the same proportion, then the auctioned item will be awarded to the user who values it the most, whose valuation is the highest.

The main problems of this auction are due to the bid shading and the sealed-bid nature of this kind of auction. In particular, when bidders' valuation are not drawn independently, i.e. when the private values information model no longer holds, this implies that there is a common value for the auctioned item. Since the auction is sealed-bid, there is no way for the bidders to estimate this and bias their bids by observing the rival bids in order to deduce on the auctioned item's market price. This, combined with the winner's curse may affect bidding behavior in the sense that bidders tend to shade a lot their bids. This shading, which may be differential among different bidders, may result in misallocation of the auctioned good and thus it is possible that no efficiency is attained.

On the other hand, this format is also beneficial if the competition in the market is low and there are asymmetries among the bidders' valuations. In such a case, the fact that bidders are unaware of their rivals' valuations usually results in more aggressive bidding and higher revenue for the auctioneer, as opposed to an open auction format.

THE DUTCH AUCTION

Presentation

This type of auction is in a sense the reverse of the English auction. Under a Dutch auction, an initial high price for the auctioned item is set. This price is gradually reduced, until a bidder claims the item. This can be done either by means of open outcry or by using a signaling protocol such as the pressing of a button, which results in stopping the price and registering the bidder as the auction winner. The price that the winner has to pay is the current auction price. That is, this is also a pay-your-bid simple auction.

Bidding Strategies

It can be seen that the strategy of the user in this auction is to decide on when to claim the auctioned item. Also, he is unaware of the rival bidders' valuations, since when that of the standing bidder is revealed the auction has by definition just ended. Therefore, essentially the game is identical, or more formally "strategically equivalent" to that of the first-price sealed-bid auction. In both auctions, the bidder without any information on the realizations of his competitors' valuation must decide on the amount of his bid. Thus, the optimal bid shading for the Dutch auction is exactly the same with that presented in the previous subsection for the first-price sealed-bid auction.

Properties

As also argued for the first-price sealed-bid auction, under the symmetric bidders model presented in the previous subsection, the auction is efficient, i.e. maximizes social welfare.

Another interesting feature, which is attractive for the seller, is that this format is not susceptible to collusion. The reason is that it is easy for a ring member to deviate and claim the auctioned item. This way, he can be awarded the auctioned item without the other ring members being able to react or exercise any punishment. This is obviously in contrast with the English auction, where the other ring members can easily respond by topping the deviating member's bid.

The aforementioned fact that the Dutch auction is *strategically equivalent* with the first-price sealed-bid auction and thus shares the same properties with it is a very strong result which is also rare in auction and mechanism design.

THE SECOND-PRICE SEALED-BID AUCTION (VICKREY)

Presentation

The second-price sealed-bid auction, is most commonly referred to as the Vickrey auction by the name of the famous economist who first proved its nice properties [7]. However, this auction has been used in practice in the Netherlands for at least 3 centuries for auctioning rare goods and performing rare stamp auctions. Like the first-price sealed-bid auction, sealed bids are submitted and the highest bid is declared as winning. However, the price that that the winner has to pay is not the price denoted in his own bid, but instead that of the second highest bid.

Bidding Strategies

Though this auction format seems a bit strange and even maybe less intuitive than the first-price sealed-bid auction, its main merit lies in the bidding strategy of the users. It is proven that under the symmetric independent private values information model, it is *dominant strategy* for the bidders to submit a bid that is equal to the respective bidder's valuation for the auctioned item.

The term dominant strategy denotes that it is always best for the bidder to place a truthful bid, regardless of what his opponents do. Note that this is a much stronger result that is also quite rare in auctions and games in general, where typically *equilibrium strategies* are computed. A certain strategy is an equilibrium strategy if the user has no incentive to deviate, i.e. to change his strategy, assuming that his rivals' strategies are fixed.

The reason behind this result is that the user's charge is both independent of his own bid and equal to the *social opportunity cost* the bidder's presence entails. This means that the bidder essentially pays the valuation of the bidder who would have become winning in the auction if the winner had not participated, that is if the winner's bid were set to zero. This charge is in fact the second highest bid submitted in the auction, i.e. the highest losing bid.

Properties

This auction, due to its sealed format, clearly suffers from all the problems regarding collusion that have been reported previously for the first-price sealed-bid auction.

An additional issue is that due to the modified payment rule, this mechanism also requires total honesty of the auctioneer. This is due to the fact that the auctioneer, in order to increase his attained revenue from the auction, and extract almost the winner's entire surplus stemming from the auctioned item's acquisition, has an incentive to insert to the auction fake bids, referred to as *phantom bids*. In particular, the auctioneer prior to announcing the bids to the bidders observes the submitted bids and inserts a fake losing bid, which is slightly lower than the winning bid. By doing do, the winner is forced to pay an amount of money which is very close to his respective valuation, thus resulting in transfer of most of his surplus to the seller.

It is worth noting that the simple Vickrey auction is equivalent to the other simple auction mechanism in terms of the auction outcome and efficiency. Under the Vickrey auction as well, it is the bidder having the highest valuation that is awarded the auctioned item.

Note also that the Vickrey auction is in a sense the sealed-bid format transformation of the English auction, with respect to the outcome and charge. In both cases, the bidder with the highest valuation is awarded the item for a charge equal to the second highest losing value, which in the English auction is revealed due to the increasing price path of the auction, while in the Vickrey auction it is submitted as a sealed bid.

Finally, despite its theoretical foundation, this mechanism is sometimes perceived as difficult and non-intuitive for inexperienced bidders. There have been field experiments with inexperienced bidders, which indicate that the users often behave irrationally, and refrain from bidding optimally, i.e. truthfully [8], [9].

SOME IMPORTANT RESULTS

This subsection provides a brief presentation of some important results of the auction theory for the simple auctions.

Revenue Equivalence Theorem

The Revenue Equivalence Theorem is one of the most fundamental results of auction theory. It is a very general result that states that any auction mechanism (actually any kind of mechanism and not necessarily an auction) where:

- all players are risk neutral,
- the player with the highest value wins,
- the player with the lowest value attains zero surplus from the mechanism,
- all values are independently drawn from the same distribution, yield

the same expected revenue to the seller.

This theorem is very powerful and defines a revenue equivalence relationship among a variety of trading mechanisms, including auctions. This relation also applies to the four aforementioned simple auction formats, namely the English auction, the Dutch auction, the first-price sealed-bid auction and the second-price sealed-bid (Vickrey) auction [4]. This theorem also ensures that the allocation of the auctioned good under all those auction mechanisms will be the same; in particular, it will be allocated to the user with the highest valuation.

It is worth emphasizing that if the bidders are not risk neutral, then the revenue equivalence theorem no longer holds. In fact, if bidders are risk averse, then for symmetric bidders with independent private values, it is proven that the ranking of the four simple auction mechanisms with respect to the revenue attained for the seller the following ranking holds:

Dutch = 1ˢᵗ-price sealed-bid > English = Vickrey

This alternative ranking of the four auction formats is due to the impact of the bidders' risk aversion on the competition exhibited.

- Under the English and Vickrey auction the bidding strategy remains the same with the one adopted if the bidders were risk neutral.
- Under the Dutch and the 1ˢᵗ–price sealed-bid auction, the risk averse bidders raise their bids in order to reduce their risk of not winning in the auction. Note that this is in sharp contrast to both the English and the Vickrey auction, where such a strategy is not beneficial. Thus under the Dutch and the 1ˢᵗ–price sealed-bid auction the competition is intensified due to the fact that bidders place higher bids in order to mitigate the risk of not being allocated the auctioned item.

Ranking of the Simple Auction Mechanism with Respect to Their Susceptibility to Collusion

A classification of the four aforementioned in this chapter auction with respect to their susceptibility to collusion, starting with the most susceptible to collusion, is as follows:

1. English auction
2. Vickrey auction
3. First-price sealed-bid auction
4. Dutch auction

The English auction is the most susceptible to collusion, since a ring member cannot deviate from the collusive bidding unobserved. This means that once he deviates, it is easy for the ring members to react by placing a higher bid; this way the deviating member will both fail to acquire the auctioned item and will not receive any side payment as ring member. Therefore, it is best for all ring members to collude.

On the contrary, collusion is not self-enforcing for sealed-bid auctions, since deviation of a collusion member is revealed only after the auction's end. Note however that this is not the case if the auction is repeated periodically.

Also, sealed-bid auctions are susceptible to other forms of dishonest dealing by dishonest auctioneers with the second-price auctions being vulnerable to auctioneer's *phantom bids* as well. On the contrary, the Dutch auction is not susceptible to any form of collusion.

Auctions and Information

We have briefly addressed the impact of information revelation by means of the auction rules to the auction outcome. It is worth emphasizing that revealing information is a two-edge sword in the context of auctions.

In particular, under the common value or affiliated values information model, the revelation of information helps bidders to bias their bids, reduces their uncertainty regarding the auctioned item's value and promotes competition and aggressive bidding. In such a context, had no information been communicated to the bidders, the latter would be very conservative in their bids, due to the *uncertainty* faced.

However, there are also some cases where revealing information is not a good idea. In particular, in cases where the competition is weak and there are large ex ante asymmetries among bidders, the English auction may perform poorly in terms of revenue.

Let us depict this by means of a simple yet somehow extreme example: Assume an item is auctioned to two bidders, one having a high value for it and one having a low value for it. This information is private information for the bidders. In case an English auction is adopted, the bidding process will reveal the second highest valuation, which is very low, thus resulting in poor revenue for the auction. On the contrary, a first-price sealed-bid auction would in general attain higher revenue, since the fear of losing would prevent the highest bidder from submitting a very low bid.

Bid Shading and Number of Bidders

So far in this chapter we have provided some basic results for the four best-known auction formats, assuming that the number of bidders participating in the auction is both known and common knowledge to the bidders. Under this assumption, the optimal bid shading of bidders drawing their valuations from a uniform distribution has been provided.

The natural question that comes up is how the optimal bid shading is computed in cases where the users are unaware of the actual number of their opponents. A second question is whether the revenue equivalence theorem still holds in this case as well. It can be proven [4] that the latter is indeed the case. This is also used to compute the optimal bidding strategy of the users in such an auction, which is defined as the weighted average of the first-price sealed-bid equilibrium bidding strategy presented earlier in this chapter for all possible realizations of number of bidders.

The former is further elaborated in the next subsection.

First-price Auctions and Number of Bidders

We have already presented the equilibrium bidding strategy of the bidders in first-price auctions earlier in this chapter. We remind the reader that in the case of the SIPV model and for valuations drawn from a uniform distribution in $[0, 1]$, this is $u \cdot \left(1 - \dfrac{1}{m} \right)$, where m is the number of bidders.

This formula provides also an intuitive explanation of why auctions are preferred and known to work well in cases of high competition. It is easy to see that in cases of low competition, the distance of the bidders' bids from their respective valuations can be quite high. In particular, assuming that there are only two bidders competing, then each user places a bid, which is half his valuation for the auctioned item.

It is interesting to compare this to a case where there are a large number of bidders competing. For instance, if there are 10 or 100 bidders competing, then users' bids are equal to the 90% and 99% of their respective valuations, under an English or first-price sealed-bid auction. Thus, the higher the competition, the closer to truth-telling the bids are.

This is a general result, which also applies to the multi-object auctions – that are to be presented in the following chapter – as well. An intuitive explanation of this is that the more competitive any market mechanism environment is and the larger the size of the market, the more "price-takers" the participants become, i.e. their individual actions are not capable of having a severe impact on the market price.

Auction Termination Point

Note that for all the auctions presented in this chapter, the termination point is not known a priori. This is not the case for many Internet auctions where "English" auctions are conducted within a predefined time interval. Note that user incentives in this case are affected by the difference in the termination rule of the auction and different bidding strategies are more meaningful for the bidders. We elaborate more on this in the remainder of this book, namely Chapter 6.

An even more "strange" rule of establishing the termination point of the auction is that of "candle auctions" [10]. Under this auction format, a short candle is lit and bidding process is terminated when it goes out. Speed is the main merit of this format, which is still used nowadays, mostly in charity wine and art auctions.

CONCLUSION

In this chapter we have presented some fundamental simple auction formats and discussed their main properties. We have presented some important concepts regarding the bidding strategies and provided a list of important results from the literature.

REFERENCES

[1]   Binmore, K. *Fun and Games: A Text on Game Theory*, Houghton Mifflin, 1991, ISBN 0-6692-4603-4.

[2]   Courcoubetis, C.; Weber R. *Pricing Communication Networks: Economics, Technology and Modelling*, John Wiley and Sons, 2003, ISBN 0-4708-5130-9.

[3]   Klemperer, P. Auction Theory: A Guide to the Literature, *Journal of Economic Surveys*, 13:3, 1999.

[4]   Krishna, V. *Auction Theory*, Academic Press, April 2002, ISBN 0-1242-6297-X.

[5]   McAfee, P.; McMillan, J. Auctions and Bidding, *Journal of Economic Literature*, 25:2, 699-738, 1987.

[6]   Wurman, P. R.; Wellman, M. P.; Walsh, W. E. A Parametrization of the
        Auction Design Space, *Games and Economic Behavior*, 35, 304-338,
        2001.
[7]   Vickrey, W. Counterspeculation, Auctions and Competitive Sealed
        Tenders, *Journal of Finance*, 16:1, 8-37, 1961.
[8]   Blumenschein, K.; Johannesson, M.; Blomquist, G.; Liljas, B.;
        O'Connor R. Hypothetical versus Real Payments in Vickrey Auctions,
        Economics Letters, 56, 177-180, 1997.
[9]   Rothkopf, M.; Teisberg, T.; Khan, E. Why are Vickrey Auctions Rare?,
        Journal of Political Economy, 98:1, 1990.
[10]   URL: http://www.answers.com/topic/candle-auctions

Chapter 3

MULTI-OBJECT AUCTIONS

ABSTRACT

This chapter is dedicated to the presentation of the most popular auction mechanisms that can be used for selling multiple objects. These objects can either be homogeneous or heterogeneous. If the latter holds, i.e. if all items are either identical or units/lots of the same good, then the multi-object auction is actually a multi-unit auction. Both multi-object and multi-unit auctions have been extensively used both in finance and telecom industry for awarding telecom resources. This chapter provides an overview of those mechanisms and discusses the pros and cons of each auction design. The material presented in this chapter, as well as additional details, can be founded by the interested reader in [1], [2], [3] and [4]. Some important results of auction theory for multi-object auctions are also presented, and a comparison of them with those presented in the previous chapter for the simple auction mechanisms is also provided.

INTRODUCTION

This chapter is a presentation of the various auction mechanisms for selling multiple objects. There are several ways to classify multi-object auctions. There are *homogeneous* and *heterogeneous* multi-object auctions, depending on the nature of the objects put up for sale. If various units of a homogeneous good are auctioned, this kind of mechanisms are said to be *multi-unit* auctions. Multi-unit auctions are extremely important since the environments in which they may be applied are of extreme practical importance (e.g. selling units of bandwidth on computer networks and satellite links, Megawatts of electric power, capacity of natural gas and oil pipelines). No surprise, the biggest part of this section deals with multi-unit auctions. A *bid* in the context of multi-unit auctions is henceforth assumed to be the *(p, q)* pair of the amount of money p offered for one unit of the item being auctioned and the desired quantity of units q, unless stated otherwise.

Moreover, the auction is said to be *combinatorial* if the submission of a unique atomic bid for combinations of objects is permitted. On the contrary, if a separate bid is required for each of the objects being auctioned, the mechanism is said to be a set of *independent* auctions. It is possible to distinguish between *simultaneous* and *sequential* auctions, whether all the goods are offered for sale simultaneously, or one after another respectively. The auction's duration is also a critical factor that provides an additional way of classification. In other words, an auction is considered to be *one-time sealed-bid* if it ends in just one round within sealed bids are accepted until a predefined time constraint is reached. It can alternatively be characterized as *progressive* if it is conducted in rounds. Last but not least, the payment rule differentiates the various mechanisms to two groups. If all the bidders pay the same price for all the goods they are awarded, the auction is said to be *uniform*, while if the charge is differentiated among the units and bidders, the auction is said to be *discriminatory*.

The literature on multi-unit auctions though relatively recent, has been growing rapidly. This chapter contains a presentation of the various mechanisms proposed and their fundamental properties. Finally, it also presents things from the seller's perspective who wants to make the most out of the auction design adopted. This way it is easier for the reader to understand the auction mechanisms and their properties, as well as why and how these were created and the context within they work best. This is extremely crucial since in slightly differentiated environments in multi-unit contexts, the same set of results cannot be applied. For instance, most results from single-unit auctions, such as the revenue equivalence theorem, still hold and can be straightforwardly for multi-unit auctions where bidders demand at most one unit. However, typically these results cannot be generalized for multi-unit auctions with bidders claiming multiple units.

GENERALIZATIONS OF SIMPLE AUCTIONS

There are many multi-unit auction mechanisms. It comes up naturally that initially such mechanisms evolved as generalizations of the single-unit auction mechanisms in an attempt to apply results and transfer experience from single-unit to multi-unit context.

In particular, the sealed-bid formats are generalized in the context of multi-object demand and supply: Multiple objects, which can be either identical or not are put up for sale and bidders are invited to submit sealed bids for them. In case identical items are auctioned, all user bids are ordered with respect to the amount of money offered and the highest of them are awarded as winning for the auctioned items. Under the first-price payment rule, each winner pays the amount of money declared in his respective winning bid for every item he is awarded.

It is worth noting that there are multiple variations of this simple format. For instance, in some auctions it is possible for the users to submit their entire demand function by means of submitting multiple sealed bids in the auction. In some formats, widely used in electricity auctions, users may bid only for discrete quantity levels; this "discretization" is typically an attempt to mitigate the potential of the bidders for manipulating the total supply in the market and thus the corresponding prices of the auction.

Moreover, it is interesting to note that if the auctioned objects are not identical, the same rules can be applied. However, it may be the case that the format is further differentiated for instance by prescribing that certain combinatorial bids may be also placed, defined by the auction's rules. An additional variation may be that the items are not put up for sale simultaneously, but they are auctioned sequentially instead, however such mechanisms are not generalizations of simple auctions and are presented later in the remainder of this chapter.

In the multi-unit context, it can be also that a uniform payment rule is applied, i.e. all winners pay the highest losing bid. That is, in an auction of N items, all winners pay for each unit awarded to them the $(N+1)^{st}$ highest bid. It is worth emphasizing that this payment rule is *not* incentive compatible and thus the multi-unit uniform-price auction is not a generalization of the single unit Vickrey auction. The remainder of this chapter elaborates more on this. In particular, the next subsection presents the generalized Vickrey auction in this context, while later we present a generalization of the English auction. Furthermore, we discuss the impact of payment rules on user incentives and thus revenue and efficiency.

We conclude the presentation of this subsection by providing a generalization of the Dutch auction for multiple identical objects, i.e. multiple "units": The general case is that of multi-unit demand, that is multiple bidders claim multiple units. Once more, a clock indicates the current market price and is initially set to a high value and gradually reduced. The units being put up for sale are reserved in exactly the same way with single-unit Dutch auction, thus instantly, and in generally different prices. The auction ends when demand matches supply, that is when all units have been claimed by and instantly awarded to the bidders. This is a popular multi-unit auction mechanism, which is mainly used in the Netherlands for selling flowers [5].

THE VCG MECHANISM

The simple Vickrey auction can be generalized for the case where multiple objects are put up for sale. The best-known generalization is the so-called **VCG** auction (Vickrey–Clarke–Groves), which as its name indicates is based on the works of Vickrey, Clarke and Groves [1]. The idea behind this mechanism is that of the simple Vickrey auction: The payment of each winner is once more defined by the respective social opportunity his presence in the auction entails: That is, user i is charged with the difference in the social welfare computed over the other agents' valuations if his own bids were set to zero. This amount is both unaffected by and less than the user's own bid. In general, this rule requires the auction to be rerun by removing each of the winners to compute his charge, resulting in general in NP complexity.

In case of multi-unit auctions, i.e. when multiple identical units of a good are auctioned, this rule is simplified to the fact that each winner pays for the kth unit he is awarded the kth highest losing bid in the auction, after his own losing bids are set to zero. Note that the exclusion of bidders' losing bids is required so that it is ensured that there is zero probability of bidders' own bids affecting his charge. This is required (yet not suffices) to ensure that incentive compatibility holds. This fact must be complemented with the rule prescribing that this independent charge is also equal to the social opportunity cost. For instance, if the auction prescribes a charge, which is independent of the user's own bids, yet lower than the social opportunity cost, then the bidder has a clear incentive to overbid. Thus, in this case the auction is not a generalized Vickrey auction and incentive compatibility no longer applies, thus possibly making it impossible for the auction to be efficient.

However, under the generalized Vickrey auction it is in the best interest of the users to truthfully reveal their valuations to the auctioneer. Therefore, the auctioned goods are awarded to the users that value them the most and efficiency is attained (social welfare maximization). Both the high computational complexity of this payment rule and the fact that a personalized charge, possibly different for different users being awarded the *same quantity* of auctioned items, are the main reasons for the limited applicability of this auction scheme in practice.

A detailed presentation of this mechanism can be found by the interested reader in [6], [7], [8] and [9]. Also in the next subsection we also present a modification of the Ascending Clock auction, which is essentially an open-format VCG auction.

THE ASCENDING CLOCK AUCTION

This auction uses an ascending clock to indicate the current pre-unit price of multiple items that are simultaneously auctioned [10]. The clock price is initially set to be ether zero or a minimum acceptable price (the *reserve price*) and is gradually incremented. For each clock price, the bidders declare the quantity of items they wish to purchase for this price. This procedure is repeated until the price for which the aggregate demand for the auctioned units becomes equal to the aggregate supply. At this point, the auctioned items are awarded to the bidders for the current clock price. The activity rule of the ascending clock auction prescribes that each bidder has to submit non-increasing bids in terms of quantity of units demanded throughout the auction.

This means that each bidder actually submits a non-increasing demand function to the auction, by reacting to the current market price. However, note that due to the fact that the payment rule is uniform, bidders do not truthfully reveal their demand function. This is thoroughly discussed in the remainder of this chapter.

THE AUSUBEL ASCENDING CLOCK AUCTION

Ausubel has proposed a variation of the ascending clock auction which overcomes this incentives problem by modifying both the allocation and the payment rule of the ascending clock auction [10]. Ausubel's ascending clock auction is based on the concept of *"clinching"*: Under this approach, units are allocated to the bidders when it becomes mathematically impossible for a user not to be awarded the allocated unit. This is intuitively translated to the fact that units are awarded to the bidders as the auction continues when the demand expressed by their opponents, i.e. the *aggregate residual demand* becomes less than the *aggregate supply* of units in the auction.

Hence, due to the fact that users are constrained to submit non-increasing bids in terms of quantity, it would be impossible for any rival bidder to claim the units "clinched", i.e. allocated to a certain bidder under a certain auction price. The price to pay for the clinched items is that of the current market price, instead of a common uniform price determined by the end point of the auction. It can be proven that this charge is essentially the social opportunity cost.

Therefore, the Ausubel's ascending clock auction is not a generalization of the English auction, but a generalization of the Vickrey auction, under an open format. Therefore, this auction combines the merits of the Vickrey auction in terms of incentive compatibility and efficiency with the advantages of an open format.

The most important advantage of this auction design is transparency due to the open format of the auction, thus preventing any kind of dishonest dealing between the auctioneer and bidders the former may wish to favor, which cannot be always guaranteed under a sealed-bid format. This is actually the main motivation behind finally adopting this scheme, after a criticized attempt to adopt a sealed-bid auction, by the government of Nigeria in order to allocate equal sized 3G spectrum licenses to cellular network operators.

Furthermore, it is worth noting that an additional advantage of this approach compared to the sealed-bid VCG auction, is that bidders reveal their demand function only up to the price of the auction termination. That is, they do not submit their entire demand function, but instead just the lower part of it up to a point. This allows the bidders not to disclose to the auctioneer and their competitors information regarding their initial high valuations. This is a very important advantage in the telecoms context, where companies do not wish to disclose such information or signal their cash liquidity to their competitors, since they can use such information in subsequent auctions for other telecom goods.

Note that all those nice features of this format are very attractive in the context of auctioning telecom licenses to wireless telecom operators. For instance, in Nigeria a sealed-bid format was initially opted for such an auction but a plethora of comments regarding the lack of transparency of the allocation procedure finally forced the government to opt for Ausubel's ascending clock auction [11].

Finally, for completeness reasons it is worth also mentioning that the Ausubel ascending auction format has also been generalized for the auctioning of heterogeneous items. However, in this "auction", the price is not necessarily modified in a monotonous way, but instead it is adapted according to a Walrasian tâtonnement process.

SOME IMPORTANT RESULTS

This subsection presents some important results of the auction theory for multi-object auctions. Some additional results are presented in the next chapter, since they motivate the design and present the tradeoffs of the design decisions for the Simultaneous Multiple Round Auction mechanism, commonly referred to in the literature as the FCC(-type) auction or the Simultaneous Ascending Auction. Also, some additional results are presented in the penultimate subsection of this chapter, as part of a discussion on how these results affect a seller's choice for adopting a certain auction mechanism.

Revenue Equivalence Theorem

The revenue equivalence theorem can be generalized, not straight forwardly though, for multi-object auctions as well. In particular, it is that all auction mechanisms, but also all means of trade, which result in the same (efficient) allocation of the auctioned goods to the bidders are revenue equivalent. The latter term is used to denote that the revenue are not exactly the same but can only differ by a constant.

It is also proven that the Vickrey Clarke Groves mechanism results in the highest revenue for the seller, among all *efficient* auction mechanisms, i.e. among all the mechanisms that award the auctioned items to the users who value them the most.

Auctions and Collusion

The ranking of the multi-object generalization of the simple auctions with respect to their vulnerability to collusion is the same with that presented for the single-unit case.

Payment Rule of Multi-Unit Auctions, Incentives and Social Welfare Maximization

Multi-unit auctions have been widely used for many decades in order to conduct auctions of billions of dollars, e.g. for financing national debt. They are also of particular importance for the telecoms sector, since they can be applied to auction e.g. units of bandwidth over a communication link. The impact of the payment rule to the bidders' incentive is of prominent importance since it greatly affects both the efficiency and the revenue attained by the auction. This issue has received considerable attention in the literature, also due to some controversial papers of the recent past. A more detailed discussion of these issues can be found in [12] and [13].

Pay-Your-Bid Payment Rule

As already discussed, under the *pay-your-bid* payment rule, bidders have a clear incentive not to bid truthfully. This is evident, since submitting truthful bids will surely result in zero net benefit for the bidder. Therefore, it is best for the bidders to submit bids, which are *lower* than their respective valuations *(bid shading)*.

This means that bidders will not truthfully report their demand function to the auctioneer. This often makes it impossible for such an auction to attain efficiency. The reason is that under some models, the percentage of the valuations' bidding is different among different units and different bids. This is called *differential bid shading*, and results to a different ranking of bidders' bids and marginal valuations. Therefore, since the auctioneer will allocate the items based on the bids, i.e. the "distorted" valuations, it is clear that in this case social welfare cannot be maximized. Also, this strategy greatly impacts the seller's attained revenue.

Uniform Price

The uniform price payment rule prescribing that all units are charged with the auctioned *cut-off price*, i.e. the highest losing bid has been quite controversial. In fact, it has even been mistakenly argued that this is the generalization of the simple Vickrey auction, thus providing incentives to bidders for truthful reporting of their valuations and correspondingly maximizing the social welfare of the auction [14]. However, this is wrong.

It has been proven that under the uniform payment rule, it is not in the interest of the bidders to truthfully report their demand function. Instead, there is a clear incentive for them to perform *demand reduction* [12], [15], [16], [17], [18], [19]. This can be seen as a special form of bid shading: This strategy prescribes that for every price for which a bid is submitted, the quantity that is demanded for this unit price should be less than the "truthful" quantity, i.e. the one derived from the bidder's demand function. The only exception to this rule is the bid for the first unit of the good auctioned, which is to be truthful.

It can also be proven that in the general case of multi-unit demand under the uniform payment rule, there is positive probability that the auction outcome is ex post inefficient, meaning that social welfare maximization is not attained. Therefore, the uniform payment rule is not a generalization of the simple Vickrey auction, as opposed to the Vickrey–Clarke–Groves mechanism, already presented previously in this chapter. We remind the reader that under the VCG rule each winner pays for the kth unit he is awarded the kth highest losing bid in the auction, after his own losing bids are set to zero, thus making truthful bidding a *weakly dominant strategy*. A question that arises is why this is the case and what is the reason that the uniform payment rule does not share this nice property.

An intuitive explanation of the motivation behind the demand reduction in the uniform price auction is that the focal weakness of the uniform payment rule is that it prescribes one *common* price for all the units awarded to each bidder, as opposed to the VCG payment rule. Therefore, under the payment rule the higher the auction cut-off price is, the higher each winner is charged for *all* the units that he has been awarded. Therefore, bidders have an incentive to try to lower that common price that they will have to pay by limiting the (aggregate) demand function in the auction. This way, the intersection point with the supply function, i.e. the auction cut-off price will be lower compared to that obtained by means of a "truthful" demand function. This is an inherent feature of the uniform payment, which according to [12] *always* results in differential bid shading. This way, the auctioned goods are not awarded efficiently.

It is worth noting though that in the somewhat theoretical case where all bidders have single-unit demand, i.e. bid for just one unit of the auctioned good, then this auction can be efficient. This is in accordance also with the fact that under the multi-unit demand case the bid for the first unit of the good is always truthful, as opposed to the bids for larger quantities. Besides the theoretical models analyzing this, such phenomena have been observed in real world auctions as well [18].

The VCG Payment Rule

It has already been explained that the generalized Vickrey auction is efficient and incentive compatible. An important result from Holstrom in [20] designates that this mechanism is the *essentially unique* auction where it is dominant strategy for the bidder to bid truthfully, the outcome maximizes social welfare and bidders having zero valuations attain zero benefit.

Note that the term «*essentially unique*» of the previous theorem implies that for any auction mechanism that has the same outcome with the generalized Vickrey auction, it can be constructed a strategically equivalent generalized Vickrey auction with the same outcome. That is, all these auctions are equivalent "definitions" of the same VCG mechanism.

A Note

The aforementioned presentation of the payment rules and their impact depicts that is quite difficult to achieve the goal of social welfare maximization under multi-unit demand. The only means by which of this can be done is a generalized Vickrey auction, under which it is dominant strategy for the bidders to bid truthfully.

DOUBLE AUCTIONS

An interesting family of multi-unit auctions is the one of *double auctions* where multiple bidders and sellers are admitted and exchange commodities. In a double auction, buyers and sellers are treated symmetrically and participate in the market by submitting *demand bids* and *supply bids* (also referred to as *offers* and *asks*) respectively. Demand and supply bids are matched in the market and market-clearing prices are generated according to some rule. The double auction is one of the most common trading mechanisms, used extensively in the various stock exchanges.

An illustrative example of a double auction is depicted above. Each horizontal line depicts a bid or an ask for one unit. Note that the highest bid in terms of the unit price is "matched" and paired with the lowest ask. This procedure is repeated until the last pair of one bid and one ask for which the bid for a unit exceeds the per-unit ask price. This is depicted with the dotted vertical line. Note that for any price within the range of these prices, it is possible to perform the transactions of the matched bids and asks which are on the left of the vertical line.

A double auction is said to be:

- *Continuous:* market is cleared at the reception of a new bid. Any seller at any time may submit an ask that is observed simultaneously by both buyers and sellers. Whenever a buyer's bid is acceptable by a seller, trade occurs.
- *Periodic:* market is cleared at a predefined time.

The most well-known mechanisms of this family are the generalization of the VCG mechanism and the Mth and $(M+1)^{st}$ clearing rules that are thoroughly presented in [4]: Assume a set of L single-unit bids of which M are sell offers and $N = L - M$ buy offers. The Mth price and $(M+1)^{st}$ clearing rule set the price at M^{th} and $(M+1)^{st}$ highest among all L bids. It is also worth noting that these price generation rules are undefined if there are no sellers or buyers respectively. The significance of these rules is that they determine the price range that balances supply and demand. Thus, every price above the Mth or less than the $(M+1)^{st}$ bid results in zero demand and supply respectively of the commodity offered and no transaction can be conducted.

Another commonly referred double auction is the *Double Dutch* auction. This mechanism is a double auction that uses two clocks as follows: The buyer clock displays the current buy price that starts high and is reduced and the seller the sell price that starts low and ascends. The auction ends when the two clocks display the same price and the market price is set at the crossing price. Buyers and sellers declare their favorable prices by stopping their clocks.

Thus pairs of buyers and sellers are gradually "locked-in" since only one clock is active: At first the buyer clock is reduced until a buyer submits a bid. Then it is stopped and the seller clock ascends until a seller submits an ask. Thus, the first buyer-seller pair is locked in and the buyer clock is resumed to descend from the price where it was stopped.

Double English is quite similar and uses two clocks as well. The difference is that the seller clock is set high while the buyer clock low. The maximum quantities that buyers and sellers would be willing to buy or sell for these prices are privately submitted and then revealed to all. Then the clocks are started and the auction ends when both display the same price, which is also set as the market price.

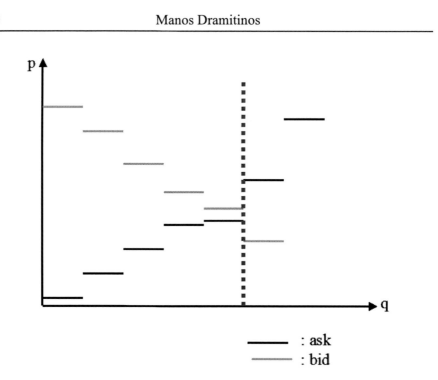

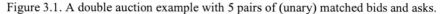

——— : ask

~~~~~ : bid

Figure 3.1. A double auction example with 5 pairs of (unary) matched bids and asks.

The Dutch English uses one clock that is set at a high price, which is reduced as time elapses. From the buyer's perspective the clock is Dutch, while from the seller's it is English. Similarly, total supply is revealed before clock starts to descend and the auction ends supply matches demand. The market price is again uniformly set to the indication of the clock.

The Double Dutch auction, as well as the Double English and Dutch English are other variations for which it is concluded that Double Dutch and Dutch English perform extremely well in terms of efficiency under a variety of market conditions.

Note that there are also simple (single-unit) double auctions. Such a simple double auction is the *k-Double auction* of Chatterjee and Samuelson [21]: A single buyer and single seller submit a bid b and ask s. If $b > s$, trade is committed at the price $kb + (1-k)s$, where k has a value between 0 and 1. The *k-Double auction* is generalized in the multi-unit context for m buyers and n sellers under single-unit demand: Each seller submits an ask and each buyer submits a bid. The $(m + n)$ asks/bids are classified in ascending order and once again there is a parameter k that has a fixed value between 0 and 1. This parameter is used as weight in order to compute the market-clearing price. In particular, this price is the weighted sums of the last matching pair's bid and respective ask. Trade occurs between bidders who bidded at least that price and sellers who asked to receive a payment at most that price.

There are several other well-known multi-unit double auctions such as the *Uniform Price Double Auction (UPDA)* where once bids and asks are submitted, the point where demand matched supply is computed and the price paid by winners is uniform.

VARIABLE QUANTITY AUCTIONS

In this subsection we briefly present on some auction formats that differ from those presented earlier in terms of the quantity of items sold. In particular, so far for all the mechanisms presented, it has been implicitly assumed that the numbered of items sold in the auction is equal to the number of items put up for auction (as long as there is demand for them). That is, the auctioneer preannounces and commits to selling a certain quantity of goods. However, there are also auction formats where such a commitment does not hold.

These auctions are referred to in the literature as *variable quantity* or *variable supply* auctions. A first reason for not committing to the quantity of auctions sold is that this is a useful to mitigate collusion and/or avoid attaining low revenue if the competition in the auction is low and an open format is opted. An additional reason is that it is always feasible for the auctioneer to improve his attained revenue by limiting the quantity of goods sold. The less the supply of goods is, the higher the prices will be. This issue has been thoroughly investigated in the theory of *optimal auctions.*

An indicative example of such an auction mechanism is a variable quantity Vickrey auction with reserve price, which has been designed by Ausubel and Cramton; see [22] for a detailed presentation. This mechanism generalizes the Vickrey auction and ensures that the allocated goods, for the quantity decided to be allocated, are assigned efficiently to the bidders. However, it is also optimal, i.e. attains the highest possible revenue for the seller. The idea is that the auctioneer decides on the quantity of goods to be sold a posteriori, i.e. after the bidders have placed their bids. In particular, the seller decides to award less than the N units auctioned. This quantity is determined by computing the revenue for all the quantities smaller than N and finally choosing the quantity that attains the highest revenue to the auctioneer.

Designing the Proper Multi-Unit Auction: A Seller's Prespective

In the previous sections of this chapter, the most important multi-unit auction mechanisms have been presented. A discussion of these mechanisms' properties and inherent features has already been provided. In this section we attempt to show how a seller, e.g. a telecom company, which wants to perform a multi-unit auction for a scarce resource, e.g. units of bandwidth of the transatlantic link connecting Europe and USA, can use these results in practice.

It is worth emphasizing that designing the proper multi-unit auction is both science and art and is in general almost impossible on arguing on the best auction format to choose without taking into account the market structure and conditions, the expected competition, and a series of factors that may affect bidder participation and strategies. However, this section is still useful in order to illustrate the impact of the various factors that greatly affect the seller in his decision to design - or choose - a suitable multi-unit auction. The presentation of the material of this section is done in an intuitive for the reader way in order to assist his comprehension of the material presented so far in this book. In particular, the impact of each design decision that a seller has to make is highlighted, its respective advantages and disadvantages are discussed, and some examples of real-world mechanisms where such decisions have been made are also provided.

Seller's Risk Aversion

A crucial parameter that has to be taken under consideration is the seller's risk aversion degree. The seller's risk aversion degree defines if he is willing to accept the fact that some of the units put up for sale may not be sold - as long as this improves his revenue. This may be plausible, though in several environments, such as privatization [23], the auction's main objective is to sell all the units with probability 1 (that is under the assumption that demand exceeds supply, a required perquisite for using any auction mechanism).

The most common tool that risk averse sellers use in order to improve revenue is the imposition of *reserve prices*: Reserve prices may be publicly announced to bidders before the auction or not. If the reserve prices are not topped by bidder's offers, these bids are considered to be losing and the corresponding units (with bids under the reserve price) remain unsold. If seller seeks to maximize the revenue attained, instead of committing to the precise quantity of the units that will be awarded to bidders, this is announced after the auction has ended and is the quantity that maximizes seller's revenue. Such a mechanism that ensures that the quantity to be finally sold is allocated efficiently and also maximizes the seller's revenue is the VCG mechanism with unknown reserve prices. To be more precise, the auction is conducted in a sealed-bid fashion and according to the rules of the VCG mechanism. At the winning phase, the bids are gathered, sorted and the seller decides to award the quantity that maximizes his revenue; this is typically less than the entire quantity available, so as to increase the social opportunity cost paid by the winners for the (fewer) units awarded to the winners. All the bids for the additional units are considered losing, thus an unknown reserve price is dynamically produced, and winners are charged according to the VCG payment rule.

The Payment Rule

The payment rule is a major decision concerning any auction design, since it greatly affects the bidders' strategy and the auction outcome. We have already presented the VCG mechanism whose success is mainly based on the clever payment rule imposed. We remind the reader that depending on the payment rule, a multi-unit auction is said to be:

- *Uniform* if all bidders pay exactly the same price for all units that have been awarded to them. This price is usually the *stop-out* price of the auction, which is the price for which demand matches supply.
- *Discriminatory* if bidders are charged in an independent fashion and pay their bid for each unit that has been awarded to them.

There has been much controversy on the literature on which payment rule is better under various contexts. As already discussed, the uniform payment rule in many cases was initially *incorrectly* considered to be the "natural" generalization of the single-unit auction in the multi-unit context ([14], [15]). Therefore, it was also argued that incentive compatible. However, as already explained earlier in this chapter, this is completely wrong, unless it is assumed that there is only single-unit demand by the bidders, i.e. all attempt to be awarded at most one unit of the good auctioned. It is often supported that it reduces winner's curse since bidders are charged in general with a lower price than their bids for all the units they are awarded, thus promoting aggressive bidding and competition. However, since the stop-out price determines the charge for *all* the units awarded, all uniform auctions suffer from *demand reduction*: Bidders submit a different demand curve than their real, demanding at every price less quantity than the one that the "honest" demand curve dictates. This is because additional units purchased raise the stop-out price, thus increasing the bidder's overall charge. Therefore these additional units reduce the bidder's net benefit and can no longer be considered as bringing positive value. The demand reduction strategy aims in keeping prices low and gaining higher payoff for fewer units of good. This way, units are misallocated and efficiency is disrupted.

This has been both proven in theory and observed in practice. Wurman et al [24] in their work also point out that *"there does not exist an individually rational, uniform-price auction with multi-unit allocations that is Bayes-Nash incentive compatible"*. In various settings, such as of low competition, zero-price equillibria are likely to appear, i.e. the users demand reduce so much that the price of the auction which must be paid by the winners is essentially zero.

Discriminatory auctions leave less space to bidders for strategic bidding. However, since bidders are aware of the fact that they pay their bids, they tend to shade their bids in order to get a discount and maintain some surplus. Empirical evidence from national debt, security and treasury auctions also support this claim, however there are cases where efficiency is not disrupted. However, it has been observed that bidders with a large market share have the advantage in discriminatory auctions [25].

Concluding, there can be no general unambiguous ranking of these auctions without making any assumptions for bidders' market power, utility functions, demand and information set.

A hybrid combining features from both the uniform and discriminatory format is the "Spanish" auction. This is a unique auction used by the bank of Spain to sell government bonds. After bid submission, the average winning bid is computed. All bids above the average are considered winning and charged with this average bid, that is ``uniformly". The winning bids below the average are charged according to the discriminatory "pay-your-bid" rule. This auction is fully presented and assessed in [26]. For a simple common-value model, it is concluded that the Spanish auction attains high revenue and is superior to the "pay-your-bid" auction.

Sealed versus Open Format

The level of market competition plays a key role in the success of any auction mechanism. This is why when designing an auction promoting competition is a major concern. It is well known that revelation of information promotes competition and aggressive bidding. This is extremely important for common-value goods. Since bidders can bias and correct their estimates based on observing the rivals bids, the fear of *winner's curse* is reduced and dynamic price discovery is achieved. Inexperienced bidders also tend to get carried away leading to even higher revenue. This is also true if the auction outcome determines the number of players in a market (e.g. telecoms) and their market power. This is why ascending auctions sometimes produce unexpectedly high revenue, e.g. at the UK UMTS auction, or the FCC auction in the US.

On the other hand, in cases of low competition ascending auctions do not work well. Under low competition and for a variety of settings and ascending auction mechanisms (an example can be found in [23]) it is proven that it is best for bidders to perform tacit collusion; that is reach an agreement early in the auction and split the units amongst them early, for a minimal payment. This results in low revenue but good efficiency, since all units are assigned to bidders with probability 1 and proportionally to their market power. That is why such mechanisms are widely in use for privatization [23]. Mitigating collusion in ascending auctions is feasible through limitation of bidder feedback and other auction-specific measures (e.g. rounding of bids).

When competition is low and the value of the units being put up for sale is not so volatile, or bidders have private values, the sealed auction formats work much better. Since there is no revelation of information, it is harder for bidders to collude. Moreover, though collusion is *self-enforcing* in most ascending auctions, this is not the case for sealed mechanisms. The uncertainty that sealed envelopes entail is a two-edged sword. On one hand, uncertainty increases the fear of winner's curse. On the other, submitting bids a bit higher than the reserve prices (if any exist) increases the probability that more units will be awarded to bidders. Also, a ring member - if collusion exists - may defect without the fear of punishment.

Sealed-bid auction mechanisms also work better if there are large ex ante asymmetries among bidders. In such a case, the ascending format results in discouraging participation of "weak" bidders. That is, if the highest value bidder is known to all a priori, then it is meaningful only for this bidder to participate in the auction. This results in zero competition and ultimately zero (or reserve) prices (as it will be discussed later in this book, several European UMTS licenses auctions suffered from this problem).

On the contrary, there is no such zero-price equilibrium under the sealed-bid format. The auction uncertainty, due to the usage of sealed envelopes, results in inefficient auction outcome and misallocation of the goods with positive probability. Hence, even weak bidders may be assigned units with positive probability, thus they have the incentive to participate in the auction.

Concluding, ascending mechanisms are more profitable if competition is high and items of undefined, common value are put up for sale. Sealed mechanisms are preferred when competition is low, collusion is highly probable and bidders have private values for the units being auctioned.

Transparency

The need for transparency is another key factor for designing an auction. If full transparency is required, so that any kind of dishonest dealing - mainly on behalf of the seller - is prevented, open, progressive auction mechanisms (ascending or Dutch) are preferred. Though collusive agreements are easier to establish in such a context, the auctioneer is unable to favor a bidder or extract larger payoffs for the units he sells. This is not the case under sealed format. Premature disclosure of information to a bidder the seller wishes to favor results in unfair treatment of bidders. Moreover, if the auction is a multi-unit generalization of the Vickrey auction, the problem of *phantom bidding* appears: The seller has the incentive to insert high "fake" losing bids in order to improve the revenue attained.

Type of Bids

The most common type of bids submitted in multi-unit auctions, is the (p, q) pair, with p being the unit price offered for each unit asked and q the quantity of units demanded. However, there are many variations of auction mechanisms depending on the type of bids submitted.

Ascending clock is an ascending mechanism where price is initially low and gradually incremented by the auctioneer. Bidders observe each price and respond by submitting the desired quantity of units. In this case, the bid is eliminated to a single number q, i.e. a declaration of the quantity desired, since it is the auctioneer who asks the price.

The activity rule enforces that the quantity q submitted by a bidder is non-increasing in consecutive rounds. With price constantly rising, bidders gradually reduce their demand and the auction terminates when demand matches supply. All bidders get the quantity they asked for and pay the stop-out price of the auction. Thus it is a uniform ascending auction, having all the problems of the ascending and uniform multi-unit auctions reported earlier.

A sealed-bid variation of the ascending clock also exists. This is a mechanism where each bidder submits his entire demand function at once in a sealed envelope. When the bidding period stops, the auctioneer opens the envelopes and constructs the aggregate demand function. By drawing a vertical line on the point Q of the total number of units being put up for sale, the aggregate function is intercepted at the point where demand matches supply and hence the stop-out price is produced.

All bids above this price are considered winning and bidders pay for all the units awarded the same stop-out price. This mechanism faces the *demand reduction* problem, lacks the *dynamic price discovery* of the ascending clock but it is hard for bidders to establish tacit collusion.

Efficiency versus Revenue

Though the standard single-unit auctions may combine efficiency with revenue maximization, this is not the case for multi-unit auctions. Efficiency (social welfare maximization) and optimality (revenue maximization) are mainly conflicting goals. In any multi-unit auction where a fixed quantity of units is to be awarded, the seller has the incentive to misallocate the units in order to maximize revenue, thus ruining efficiency.

It is important that the reader does not confuse efficiency with the revenue attained. For example, in the Finnish UMTS auction the Finish government decided to award all the licenses to the country's major telecom operators without any (significant) charge, since these industries were best able to use these licenses.

Even when revenue maximization is not the primary goal, applying a pay-your-bid payment rule often results in differentiated bid shading and applying a uniform payment rule leads to demand reduction.

In both cases, social welfare is not maximized in general. Only the VCG payment rule preserves efficiency. In order to combine it with optimality the quantity to be awarded to bidders must remain uncertain, as already stated previously in this section.

CONCLUSION

In this chapter we have presented some fundamental multi-object auction formats and discussed their main properties. Some important results regarding the bidding strategies and how they are affected by the auction payment rule have been provided. An additional list of important results from the literature has also been presented and the tradeoffs in multi-object auction mechanism design decisions have been highlighted.

REFERENCES

[1]   Binmore, K. *Fun and Games: A Text on Game Theory*, Houghton Mifflin, 1991, ISBN 0-6692-4603-4.

[2]   Courcoubetis, C.; Weber R. *Pricing Communication Networks: Economics, Technology and Modelling*, John Wiley and Sons, 2003, ISBN 0-4708-5130-9.

[3]   Wolfstetter, E. *Topics in Microeconomics*, Cambridge University Press, 1999.

[4]   Wurman, P. R.; Wellman, M. P.; Walsh, W. E. A Parametrization of the Auction Design Space, *Games and Economic Behavior*, 35, 304-338, 2001.

[5]   Kambil, A; van Heck, E.: Reengineering the Dutch Flower Auctions: A Framework for Analyzing Exchange Organizations. *Information Systems Research*, 9(1): 1-19 (1998).

[6]   Blumenschein, K.; Johannesson, M.; Blomquist, G.; Liljas, B.; O'Connor R. Hypothetical versus Real Payments in Vickrey Auctions, *Economics Letters*, 56, 177-180, 1997.

[7]   Dasgupta, P.; Maskin, E. Efficient Auctions, *Quarterly Journal of Economics*, 115:2, 341-388, 2000.

[8]   Jehiel, P.; Moldovanu, B. Efficient Design with Interdependent Valuations, *Econometrica*, 69:5, 1237-1259, 2001.

[9]   Krishna, V. *Auction Theory*, Academic Press, April 2002, ISBN 0-1242-6297-X.

[10]   Ausubel, L., An Efficient Ascending-Bid Auction for Multiple Objects, *American Economic Review*, 94:5, 1452-1475, 2004.

[11]   Lee, D. Lessons from the Nigerian GSM Auction, *Telecommunications Policy*, 27, 407-416, 2003.

[12]   Ausubel L.; Cramton, P. , Demand Reduction and Inefficiency in Multi-Unit Auctions, University of Maryland, Working paper No. 96-07, revision 2002. URL:http://www.ausubel.com/auction-papers.htm

[13]   Binmore K.; Swierzbrinski, J. Treasury Auctions: Uniform or Discriminatory?, *Review of Economic Design*, 5, 387-410, 2000.

[14]   Miller, M. *New York Times*, 3:13, 15 September1991.

[15]   Nautz, D.; Wolfstetter, E. Bid shading and Risk Aversion in multi-unit auctions with many bidders, *Economics Letters*, 56, 195-200, 1997.

[16]   Nautz, D.; Wolfstetter, E. Optimal Bids in Multi-Unit Auctions When Demand is Price Elastic, *Mimeo*, March 1996.

[17]   Tenorio, R. Multiple Unit Auctions with Strategic Price-Quantity Decisions, *Economic Theory*, 13, 247-260, 1999.

[18]   Tenorio, R. Revenue Equivalence and Bidding Behavior in a Multi-Unit Auction Market: *An Empirical Analysis, Review of Economics and Statistics*, 75:2, 302-314, 1993.

[19]   Tenorio, R. Some Evidence on Strategic Quantity Reduction in Multiple Unit Auctions, *Economics Letters*, 55, 209-213, 1997.

[20]   Holmstrom, B. Grove's Scheme on Restricted Domain, *Econometrica*, 48:5, 1137-1144, 1979.

[21]   Chatterjee, K.; Samuelson, W. Bargaining under Incomplete Information, *Operations Research*, 31, 835-51.

[22]   Ausubel L.; Cramton, P., Vickrey Auctions with Reserve Pricing, *Economic Theory*, 23, 493-505, 2004.

[23]   Menezes, F. Multiple-unit English auctions, *European Journal of Political Economy*, Vol. 12, pp. 671-684, 1996.

[24]   Wurman, P. R.; Wellman, M. P.; Walsh, W. E. Flexible Double Auctions for Electronic Commerce: Theory and Implementation, *Univ. of Michigan Working paper*, 1998.

[25]   Bower, J. and Bunn, D. Experimental analysis of the efficiency of uniform-price versus discriminatory auctions in the England and Wales electricity market. *Journal of Economic Dynamics and Control*, 25, pp. 561-592, 2000.

[26]   Abbink, K. ; Brandts, J. and Pezanis-Christou, P. Auctions for government securities: A laboratory comparison of uniform, discriminatory and Spanish designs, *Journal of Economic Behavior and Organization*, Elsevier, vol. 61(2), pages 284-303, October 2006.

Chapter 4

THE FCC AUCTION:
DESIGN AND APPLICATIONS

ABSTRACT

This chapter presents the FCC auction, which has been extensively used in the United States of America for the allocation of spectrum licenses to wireless telecom providers. The main design decisions are discussed and some related results from auction theory that affected the final design are provided. As part of this discussion, some additional results of auction theory regarding multi-object auctions are provided. The practical applications of the FCC auction and some indicative results are also presented, as well as an identification of the main types of bids and strategies observed. Additional studies of instance of auctions for spectrum licenses, which have taken place in Europe as opposed to the auctions presented in this chapter, are provided in the next chapter.

INTRODUCTION

This chapter presents the FCC (or FCC-type) auction, whose official name is the Simultaneous Multiple Round Auction [1]. An academic name used to refer to this type of auction is the Simultaneous Ascending Auctions; both terns are used interchangeably throughout the remainder of this book chapter.

This auction mechanism was designed in the United States of America for allocating chunks of the publicly owned radio spectrum to wireless telecom operators for a variety of wireless network technologies and services, ranging from narrowband to broadband [2]. This auction design was ordered from the

U.S. Federal Communications Commission (FCC) in order to allocate the radio spectrum in the form of licenses: Each license pertains to the right of exclusive use of a certain frequency band over a geographical area for a very long period of time, typically 20-30 years [3]. This auction has been considered as a huge success, since its outcome resulted in significant revenue for the state and performed very well in terms of the social welfare attained; see [2], [4], [5], and [6]. This form of auctioning spectrum is in sharp contrast with the procedure of comparative hearings or lotteries used before, which was a tedious bureaucratic procedure lacking transparency and any economic or technological merits.

The prominent goal of this auction is *social welfare maximization*. It is very important for the scarce radio spectrum to be utilized by the telecom operators that value it the most, and thus can use it in the most efficient way to provide the best services to the customers in the most cost-effective way. Attaining *high revenue* for the state is also an important complementary goal of this auction. This is important in order to compensate for the use of a scarce public resource for commercial purposes and it comprises further evidence that the competition in the market has been fierce enough to advocate for an auction-based allocation scheme. An equally important goal that this auction design was also obliged to meet is transparency in the allocation procedure.

As the name Simultaneous Multiple Round auction indicates, under this auction format multiple licenses are auctioned simultaneously in multiple rounds, starting from a low reserve price, which can be in general different per license. Bidders place independent, i.e. non-combinatorial bids for the licenses of interest by means of sealed tenders at every auction round. Upon the bid submission phase deadline of each round is reached, no more bids are accepted and some feedback is sent to the bidders, which is at least the standing bid and bidder for every license. The minimum acceptable for the next round is also announced, which is the current standing bid plus a *bid increment*. Bids for a license that do not exceed this sum are not considered to be *valid*.

The auction rules are complemented by rules prescribing the minimum amount of bids that each bidder should place at every round of the auction (*activity rule*), which also determines the maximum number of licenses he is eligible to claim (*eligibility rule*). These rules also define how bidder's eligibility is reduced in cases where he fails to meet the activity rule requirements.

The auction is over when there is a round for which no new bid was submitted for any of the auctioned licenses.

It is worth noting that since all licenses are auctioned simultaneously, bidders can freely change the licenses they bid for until the auction is ended. A more detailed presentation of the auction rules, which were also different among different instances of this auction, is to be provided in the remainder of this chapter.

The steps taken before the initiation of an auction are also interesting. Typically these comprise of public hearings and consultations, setting rules for who is eligible to take psrt in the auction, depositing upfront payments and presenting bank guarantees so that the bidders can prove their credibility, running mock auctions for training purposes. The thorough presentation of this sequence of auction preparation steps is beyond the scope of this book. The interested reader may refer to [7] for a thorough presentation.

AUCTION RATIONALE

This subsection briefly presents the auction rationale, i.e. is a justification of the major design decisions that were taken regarding the format and the rules of the auction. A detailed presentation of the issues discussed here can be found in [2].

The first thing to be decided was if the auction format should be *open* or *sealed-bid*. An open format was opted, with the main reasons being:

- The fact that a big part of the value of the spectrum licenses to be auctioned is common for all the bidders. Therefore, information should be revealed so that the fear of winner's curse is mitigated and aggressive bidding is promoted.
- The failure of sealed-bid formats to attain efficiency and high revenue in many similar cases, such as the New Zealand auction [2].
- The goal of transparency, in order to make it impossible for any kind of dishonest dealing clearly motivated an open format.

Another major choice was whether the licenses would be auctioned one after another, i.e. *sequentially*, or instead *simultaneously*. The supporters of the first approach claimed that it is a widely used practice – mostly in wine and timber auctions – which is not vulnerable to *collusion*. The supporters of the latter claimed that only a simultaneous auction format would allow bidders to choose the licenses they pursue by reacting to the current standing prices and eventually form combinations of licenses that they truly desire.

The latter is very important since the acquisition of adjacent licenses in terms of geographical region or frequency bands exhibits strong *complementarities*. That is, the value of a license is higher if neighboring licenses are also acquired (*synergistic effect*). Neighboring licenses in terms of geographical coverage are useful to provide seamless roaming and establish a strong customer base over a larger geographical region. Neighboring licenses in terms of frequency, i.e. adjacent frequency bands can be utilized more efficiently since the FCC rules prescribe that for each license there is a guard band that cannot be utilized so as to prevent interference with other networks; obviously, if neighboring bands belong to the same wireless telecom provider, the guard bands can be utilized to provide services as well, thus increasing the quantity of the holder's spectrum.

A sequential auction would not take into account this fact and bidders would be essentially deterred from expressing such complementarities by means of aggressive bidding in the auctions. On the other hand, the simultaneous format, which was opted, inherently suffers from the *exposure problem*, which is described later in this chapter.

Another phenomenon of sequential auctions that prevented it from being adopted is the so-called *declining price anomaly*. This term is used to describe the increasingly higher decline of prices in subsequent auctions, due to the drop in competition. A prominent example of auction where this phenomenon was evident was the RCA telecom satellite channels auction in 1981 [6]. In this sequential auction, prices were significantly reduced in subsequent auctions and to make matters worse, this was considered to be illegal due to fact that the regulatory regime of the time prescribed that the market price of identical telecom goods cannot exhibit large differences. This resulted in the a posteriori enforcement of a low uniform charge for all the auction winners, further reducing the attained revenue. This also favored the FCC decision to simultaneously auction all the available licenses.

A more ambiguous decision had to be made regarding whether *package (combinatorial) bids* should be allowed or not. Supporters of the combinatorial bids claimed that it was the only way to deal effectively with the *exposure problem*, while those in favor of independent bids argued in terms of the higher complexity of the combinatorial approach and also that the combinatorial bids would lead to the *free rider* and *threshold* problem; these are presented later in this chapter. Finally, FCC initially opted for individual bids, however it has recently also experimented in some auctions to allow combinatorial bids as well.

Finally, it was opted for the auction to comprise a series of *discrete rounds*, rather than being *continuous* in order for the bidders to have time to process the auction feedback and also assess and plan their strategies. The use of *minimum bid increments* and the *eligibility* and *activity* rules aim to speed up the auction.

AUCTION RULES

The most typical set of rules of the FCC auction, since there are multiple variations and differences among various executions, are as follows:

1. All the licenses are simultaneously auctioned.
2. Each bidder can claim any license as long as he is not prohibited from his *eligibility rule*.
3. The auction is terminated if for some round there are not any new valid bids submitted in the auction.
4. Depending on the auction, there may apply *quantity restrictions* regarding the maximum number of telecom assets that a company may possess over a geographical region. These restrictions stem from the regulatory competition laws framework and apply to the auction.
5. It is possible to mark certain licenses where certain bidders, referred to as *Designated Entities*, that belong to certain community groups (e.g. minorities) have preferential treatment, i.e. obtain a discount, as opposed to the rival bidders.
6. Bidders must deposit a significant amount of money as *upfront payment*, which also determines the size and number of licenses they are eligible to pursue. Also, auction winners must deposit the remaining amount of money they have to pay for the licenses awarded within a short time period after the auction is ended, otherwise they lose the right to own the licenses awarded to them by means of the auction.
7. At every round of the auction, the auctioneer announces a *minimum bid increment* that defines the minimum amount of money above which a new bid for a license is considered to be a valid bid.
8. In general, the auction comprises of three *stages*. Each stage corresponds to a minimum activity of the bidders so that their

eligibility is not reduced. If a bidder is below his minimum activity level, he may use up to five *waivers* and subsequently his eligibility is gradually reduced,

9. The number of rounds per day is decided by the auctioneer and is subject to change only by him; so is the duration of each round.

10. The identities of the bidders and round winners are publicly announced. The only exception to that rule is the Nationwide Narrowband Auction, where instead of the company name an abstract id was announced. This change was made in an attempt to limit bidders to take into advantage the prior announcements of the companies regarding the licenses that they wished to be allocated in order to "share" among them the auctioned licenses and keep the prices low. However, this rule was later aborted since bidders were actually coding their identities as part of their bids and it was also very easy to deduce on which company corresponded to what id given the footprint of the licenses it was trying to acquire.

11. After the bidding phase of each round, there is a small withdrawal phase during which a bidder may withdraw some of his bids. If the withdrawn bid is a standing bid for a license, then there is a monetary fine to be paid.

This is an indicative set of rules. In practice, there were multiple variations of the above rules plus introduction of new rules in cases where it was considered beneficial to do so sue to the nature of the licenses and the expected competition.

SOME RELATED AUCTION THEORY RESULTS

This subsection presents some auction theory results that motivated the FCC auction design, as well as some that seem to contradict some of the design's rationale. More details can be found by the interested reader in [8], [9], [10], [11] and [12].

Exposure Problem

This is a problem that appears both in FCC auctions and any type of multi-object auctions where combinatorial bids are not allowed. In particular, a bidder pursuing a combination of goods (e.g. licenses) plays independent bids for each one of them. Due to the complementarities from the acquisition of the package of licenses, the bidder may be willing to bid for each one of them more than its individual value to him. Therefore, if the bidder fails to win some of the pursued goods due to the high prices, he may end up having paid more for some licenses than their value. Besides the negative net benefit, an additional problem is that by getting those licenses that are not of high value to him, he prohibits the allocation of these licenses to the users who indeed value them the most, thus also disrupting the social welfare attained.

Threshold Problem

This is a problem that appears if combinatorial bids are placed. Assume the case of a combinatorial bid for e.g. 2 items that is higher than the sum of the two standing bids in these licenses. Also assume that this combinatorial bid is *not* higher than these two players' valuations, and that none of the two bidders cannot displace the combinatorial bid unilaterally. Therefore, since none of the user has the incentive to place a "losing" bid for each of the auctioned goods, the combinatorial bid becomes the standing bid in the auction, which is clearly inefficient.

Strategic Manipulation

This is also a problem that appears in combinatorial auctions. In particular, in such auctions it is custom that the auction rules prescribe that combinatorial bids are preferred compared to one-item bids. This provides an incentive to users to create packages of the desired items – where the competition may be high – with other items of low value and placing a combinatorial bid for all of them. Thus, by taking into account the threshold problem, such users get allocated licenses that they are not interested in along with those that they desire but should have been allocated elsewhere if social welfare were to be maximized.

Collusion

Since the format of the FCC auction is open, it facilitates (implicit) collusion among the bidders. An easy way that users can collude is by doing "gift withdrawals": a bidder may withdraw from some license(s) that one of their rivals wants so that the latter also stops competing against that bidder for other licenses of interest. The large amount of information and the multiple round format of the auction clearly facilitate this strategy, which has been observed in practice. Note that this result is also in line with the discussion regarding the impact of information on collusion in previous chapters of this book.

Fairness

McAffee and McMillan [13] address the issue of whether it is acceptable or not for licenses that are identical to be allocated under different prices. Luckily, the FCC auction performed well in terms of fairness, as will also be shown in the remainder of this chapter.

INDICATIVE AUCTION INSTANCES

This subsection contains three indicative auctions conducted by the FCC in the USA, which have been subject to extensive analysis and discussion in the literature. Note that detailed data about all the FCC auctions conducted are publicly available in the FCC website [1] and other similar sites [14]. An excellent detailed analysis can also be found in [5], [6], and [8].

Nationwide Narrowband (PCS) Auction

Auction Description
This is the first Simultaneous Multiple Round auction conducted by the FCC [15]. Ten licenses were auctioned to 29 qualified bidders.

The licenses auctioned were not identical: 5 were licenses for symmetric paired spectrum 50/50kHz, 3 asymmetric pairs 50/12.5kHz and 2 of 50kHz.

As the auction name indicates, the licenses were of nationwide coverage and suitable for PCS (paging) services.

The auction took place in the time period 25-29 July 1994 and comprised 47 rounds.

Bidding Strategies and Auction Outcome

This is an auction where the competition exhibited was very high throughout the auction. Bidders tried to acquire neighboring licenses (in terms of frequency) so that they could take advantage of the utilization of the guard band. This is also evident in the final allocations of the auction results provided later in this subsection. Bidding was aggressive and there were not any withdrawals, which along with the fact that neighboring licenses were awarded to the same bidder, indicate that bidders did not suffer from the *exposure problem* and managed to create efficient combinations of licenses.

The final auction results are provided below. It is clear that the price of same type licenses is similar and "proportional" to the respective license size. This comprises an additional evidence of the efficiency of the auction.

Nationwide Narrowband PCS Auction		
License	**Winner**	**Winning Bid**
N-1 50/50kHz Paired	**Paging Network of Virginia**	**$80.000.000**
N-2 50/50kHz Paired	**Paging Network of Virginia**	**$80.000.000**
N-3 50/50kHz Paired	**KDM Messaging Company**	**$80.000.000**
N-4 50/50kHz Paired	**KDM Messaging Company**	**$80.000.000**
N-5 50/50kHz Paired	**Nationwide Wireless Network Corp.**	**$80.000.000**
N-6 50/12.5kHz Paired	**Airtouch Paging**	**$47.001.001**
N-7 50/12.5kHz Paired	**Bell South Wireless**	**$47.505.673**
N-8 50/12.5kHz Paired	**Nationwide Wireless Network Corp.**	**$47.505.000**
N-9 50KHz Unpaired	**Nationwide Wireless Network Corp. (Pioneer License Allocation)**	**$33.300.000**
N-10 50KHz Unpaired	**Paging Network of Virginia**	**$37.000.000**
N-11 50KHz Unpaired	**Pagemart II, Inc.**	**$38.000.000**

Figure 4.1. The results of the Nationwide Narrowband PCS auction.

Competition was fierce throughout the auction, with bidders alternating between the three types of licenses when the prices at every such "market" were too high. This is also depicted in the following graph:

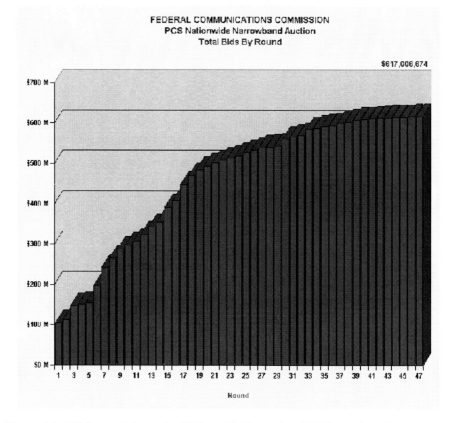

Figure 4.2. Bidding activity in the Nationwide Narrowband PCS Auction. Source: http://wireless.fcc.gov/auctions/01/charts/1_cht1.gif.

It is worth noting that in this auction, the bidders adopted *jump bidding* frequently. The term *jump bidding* is used to denote the placement of a bid that is much higher than the minimum valid bid for a license. The idea behind this is that placing a very high bid is supposed to signal the determination of a bidder to acquire the specific licenses and deter competition of his rivals. In practice, due to the intense competition, this action only impacted the speed of the auction, which was concluded within 5 days. Note that this is in sharp contrast with the previous methods of comparative hearings and lotteries. The latter tedious allocation procedures involved years of negotiations and also possible legal actions of parties who were excluded from the final allocation.

The total revenue attained were a magnitude of order higher than those that FCC had originally estimated. This helped a lot in the adoption of this format for the subsequent auctions to be held by the FCC. Also, efficiency was attained and market prices per license type evolved through the ascending price format of the auction.

Regional Narrowband PCS Auction

Auction Description

This auction was held in the time period of October 26th 1994 to November 8th 1994. The frequency bands allocated are similar to those allocated by means of the Nationwide Narrowband PCS Auction presented in the previous subsection, in the sense that it is also useful for the provision of PCS (paging) services. As opposed to the Nationwide Narrowband PCS Auction, the licenses of the Regional Narrowband PCS Auction were not nationwide: the US region was divided to 5 geographical regions, depicted in the figure below. Within every region, 6 frequency bands (licenses) were auctioned. Thus, a total of 30 licenses were auctioned. There were 9 auction winners and the total duration of the auction was 105 rounds.

An immediate implication of this auction is that its model is more complicated than that of the Nationwide Narrowband PCS Auction, due to the fact that the licenses auctioned can be neighboring both in terms of frequency band and geographical region. 28 telecom companies participated in this auction and 9 of them were winners, i.e. they were allocated licenses.

It is also worth noting that this auction is preceded from the Nationwide Narrowband Auction in time. This implies that the Regional Narrowband PCS Auction essentially comprised the last chance of telecom providers of PCS services to acquire the required spectrum for conducting their business either in regional or nationwide level.

Similarly to the Nationwide Narrowband Auction, there was intense competition in this auction. The first stage of the auction consists of the first 20 rounds. Rounds 21 to 74 comprise the auction's second stage, while rounds 75 to 105 the third (final) stage.

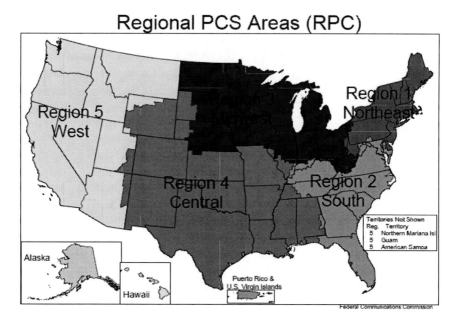

Figure 4.3. The geographical regions of the Regional Narrowband PCS Auction.
Source: http://wireless.fcc.gov/auctions/data/maps/rnpcs.pdf.

Bidding Strategies and Auction Outcome

The dominant bidding strategy in this auction was aggregation of neighboring licenses. In particular, bidders clearly tried – and the most powerful of them succeeded to a large extent – to acquire licenses of neighboring frequency bands and over neighboring geographical regions. Some bidders clearly desired to form a nationwide network by bidding on the same frequency band over all the regions, or alternatively over the regions where they had not already established presence before.

The auction outcome is depicted in the table below: Note that frequency bands 2 and 6 are marked with an asterisk to depict that these frequency bands had been marked as Designated Entities Licenses. This means that certain companies that fulfilled certain social requirements (representing minorities, women groups etc.) identified by the legislation as Designated Entities had the right to attain a predefined discount over the final prices of these licenses. This discount was significantly high; it comprised the 40% of the bidded price. In fact, the companies that were awarded these frequency bands were indeed Designated Entities, but the prices of these licenses were approximately 40% higher than that of neighboring frequency bands. However, the identification of the designated entity licenses promoted competition in the auction, since designated entities formed joint companies that bidded aggressively for those licenses. An additional common feature in terms of the bidding strategies observed with the Nationwide Narrowband PCS Auctions, is that in this auction as well there was a significant amount of jump bidding performed.

Band	Type (kHz)	LICENCE WINNERS				
		NorthEast	South	MidWest	Central	West
1	50/50	Pagemart II Inc.				
2*	50/50	PCS Development Corporation				
3	50/12.5	Mobile Media PCS Inc.				
4	50/12.5	Advanced Wireless Messaging Inc.				
5	50/12.5	AirTouch Paging	InstaCheck Systems Inc.	Ameritech Mobile Serrvices	AirTouch Paging	
6*	50/12.5		Lisa-Gaye Shearing		Benbow PCS Ventures Inc.	

Figure 4.4. The outcome of the Regional Narrowband PCS Auction.

In fact, PCS Development submitted such high bids for the frequency band 2 nationwide that were never displaced and also were higher than the winning bids in neighboring frequencies.

The main strategies observed in this auction are:

- Forming aggregations of neighboring licenses.
- Break-up of the aggregations of the rival bidders. It was attempted from certain companies to break their rivals aggregations so as to limit these companies strength in the market.
- Fake demand over some licenses so as to drive prices up there and then shift to claiming the licenses of interest.
- Bidders who were interested in being awarded just one license somewhere attempted to punish rival bidders elsewhere so that they would perform a gift withdrawal of some license to them. This strategy did not pay off in practice, mostly due to the fact that it was

adopted by bidders of low budget who at the best case simply raised the price to pay for the standing bidders.

The bidding activity and revenue graph of the auction is depicted below:

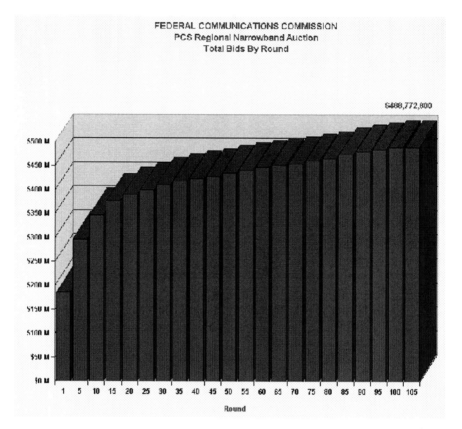

Figure 4.5. The revenue graph of the Regional Narrowband PCS Auction. Source: http://wireless.fcc.gov/auctions/03/charts/3_cht1.gif.

It is worth noting that the final outcome of the auction is identical to that observed in the 7th round. This seemingly strange phenomenon is actually common in many FCC auctions. Its explanation is that once prices go up, i.e. towards the end of the auction, bidders tend to bid over those few licenses that they value the most: These licenses are also the licenses where they place their initial bids early in the auction, when the eligibility rule demands that a few number of bids are to be submitted in the auction.

Major Trading Areas (MTA) Broadband PCS Auction

Auction Description

As the name of this auction indicates, the spectrum licenses put up for sale are suitable for the provision of broadband services. In this auction, the geographical coverage of the licenses auctioned were significantly smaller compared to that in the previous two auctions described earlier in this chapter. In particular, the US was divided to 51 regions, formally stated as Major Trading Areas (MTA). For each MTA, two 30MHz spectrum licenses were auctioned. This is why this auction is also commonly referred to as Broadband PCS A and B Block Auction. As opposed to the Regional Narrowband PCS Auction, there were not any designated entities/licenses in this auction.

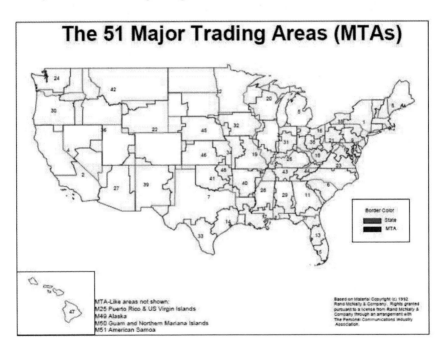

Figure 4.6. The partitioning of the U.S. in 51 Major Trading Areas for the MTA Broadband PCS Auction. Source: http://wireless.fcc.gov/auctions/data/maps/mta.pdf

The partitioning of the US in 51 major trading areas is depicted in the figure below. Note that the definition of the trading areas does not coincide with the state borders. In particular, in all the auctions conducted, the definition of a meaningful license is far from trivial. In general, different areas of the country exhibit huge differences in terms of population density, average income, wealth of people in neighboring states, competition level etc. For instance, the population density and average income in Manhattan is much different than that of a rural state. Also, the infrastructure costs required for the wireless telecom provider to supply services there are very different.

Therefore, it is important in order to promote completion for the licenses auctioned, to ensure that these are defined in such a way that they are viable and attractive for service provisioning in market terms. Obviously this comprises an additional overhead for the auctioneer; however the FCC auction merits and its superiority compared to other means of allocating the licenses clearly indicate that this is something worth doing.

This auction was conducted in the time period between the December 5th 1994 and March 13th 1995. There were 60 bidding days and the auction comprised of 112 rounds. 30 qualified bidders participated in this auction 18 out of the 30 qualified bidders were winners. The attained revenue was approximately $7 billion. Large alliances among telecom companies were formed, which along with the competition laws that prescribe that a certain company cannot have more than a certain amount of telecom holdings over a certain area resulted in having few bidders competing over a certain region. For instance, AT&T was not eligible to bid for the 48% of the licenses auctioned.

Bidding Strategies and Auction Outcome

The auction was conducted in three stages. Stage 1 began in round 1 and was concluded in round 11. Stage 2 began in round 12 and was concluded in round 64. Stage 3 began at round 65 and was concluded in round 112. As clearly indicated by the activity and revenue graph below, the FCC's decision to change stage in round 12 was clearly motivated by the limited bidding activity and it helped to boost competition in the auction. An indicative table of results depicting the highest bids and top markets by population are depicted below. It can be seen that prices among different regions vary a lot. For instance, the licenses of New York or Los Angeles exhibit very high prices. The detailed results of the auction can be found online in [16]. The main strategies in this auction were *geographical strategies*: These strategies were adopted by established companies who saw this auction as an opportunity to enter the markets of neighboring geographical regions to areas where they already were active. A big number of companies actually managed to make such meaningful combinations of licenses that were complementary to their presence in other US areas.

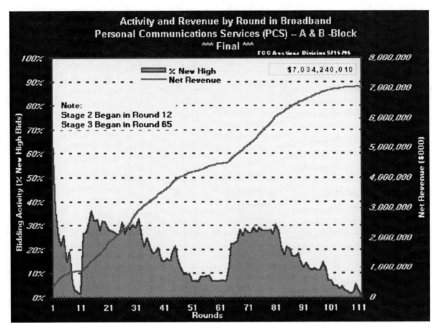

Source: http://wireless.fcc.gov/auctions/04/charts/4_cht1.gif.

Figure 4.7. Activity and revenue by round.

Federal Communications Commission PCS A & B - Block Auction ***Final***									
*** F i n a l R e s u l t s ***									
Auction Closed in Round		112		Net Revenue: $7,034,240,010					

Top 10 High Bids by Bid Size					Top 10 Markets by Population				
MTA	BTA	Market	Round	Current High Bidder	Net High Bid	MTA	BTA	Market	Pop (000's)	Current High Bidder	Net High Bid
2	B	Los Angele	82	Pacific Telesis Mobile Ser	$493,500,000	1	B	New York	26,411	WirelessCo, L.P.	$442,712,000
1	B	New York	74	WirelessCo, L.P.	$442,712,000	2	B	Los Angele	19,145	Pacific Telesis Mobile Ser	$493,500,000
3	B	Chicago	77	PCS PRIMECO, L.P.	$385,050,583	3	A	Chicago	12,070	AT&T Wireless PCS Inc.	$372,750,000
3	A	Chicago	75	AT&T Wireless PCS Inc.	$372,750,000	3	B	Chicago	12,070	PCS PRIMECO, L.P.	$385,050,583
10	B	Washingto	77	AT&T Wireless PCS Inc.	$211,771,000	4	A	San Franci	11,891	WirelessCo, L.P.	$206,500,000
4	A	San Franci	98	WirelessCo, L.P.	$206,500,000	4	B	San Franci	11,891	Pacific Telesis Mobile Ser	$202,150,000
4	B	San Franci	97	Pacific Telesis Mobile Ser	$202,150,000	5	A	Detroit	10,001	AT&T Wireless PCS Inc.	$81,177,000
11	A	Atlanta	89	AT&T Wireless PCS Inc.	$198,411,000	5	B	Detroit	10,001	WirelessCo, L.P.	$96,107,000
11	B	Atlanta	87	GTE Macro Communicatic	$184,660,483	6	A	Charlotte	9,752	AT&T Wireless PCS Inc.	$66,616,000
15	A	Miami	88	WirelessCo, L.P.	$131,723,000	6	B	Charlotte	9,752	BellSouth Personal Comn	$70,907,001

Top 10 Bidders by Dollar Value of High Bids			Top 10 Markets by Net $/pop					
Bidder Name	Net $ of High Bids	# of High Bids	MTA	BTA	Market	Net $/pop	Current High Bidder	Net High Bid
WirelessCo, L.P.	$2,110,079,168	29	3	B	Chicago	$31.90	PCS PRIMECO, L.P.	$385,050,583
AT&T Wireless PCS Inc.	$1,694,418,000	21	3	A	Chicago	$30.88	AT&T Wireless PCS Inc.	$372,750,000
PCS PRIMECO, L.P.	$1,107,226,000	11	11	A	Atlanta	$28.58	AT&T Wireless PCS Inc.	$198,411,000
Pacific Telesis Mobile Services	$695,650,000	2	24	A	Seattle	$27.79	GTE Macro Communicatic	$106,355,002
GTE Macro Communications Co	$398,251,451	4	24	B	Seattle	$27.48	Windsong Communication	$105,163,484
American Portable Telecommuni	$288,872,034	8	10	B	Washingto	$27.23	AT&T Wireless PCS Inc.	$211,771,000
Ameritech Wireless Communical	$158,100,000	2	11	B	Atlanta	$26.60	GTE Macro Communicatic	$184,660,483
Western PCS Corporation	$144,208,262	6	2	B	Los Angele	$25.78	Pacific Telesis Mobile Ser	$493,500,000
Powertel PCS Partners, L.P.	$124,447,000	3	15	A	Miami	$25.64	Windsong Communication	$131,723,000
PhillieCo. L.P.	$84,995,012	1	19	A	St. Louis	$25.48	AT&T Wireless PCS Inc.	$118,936,000

C Auctions Division: 5/16/96

Source: http://wireless.fcc.gov/auctions/04/charts/4_cursum.gif

Figure 4.8. Some indicative auction results.

Moreover, most bidders opted to bid for the minimum number of licenses required by the activity rule so that the bidder's eligibility is not reduced. As opposed to the Narrowband Auctions, there was very limited use of jump bidding since the limited number of competitors per licenses increased the risk of submitting an erroneously high jump bid.

Types of Bids

From the aforementioned presentation of FCC auctions, it can be seen that there are the following types of bids in the FCC auctions:

- *Sincere bids:* These are the bids that are placed by the bidder at the licenses where given the current prices will result to maximizing his net benefit. The amount of money bidded for these licenses equals the current standing bid of that license plus the minimum bid increment.
- *Jump bids:* Placement of very high bids in order to signal the bidder's determination to acquire a certain license or group of licenses. In practice, if the auction is competitive enough, bidders are mostly affected by prices rather than this kind of signaling. These bids are only beneficial if the competition is low and there is a big partitioning of licenses so that there are multiple substitute licenses for the bidders. In such a case, the bidders can use this type of bids to reach a consensus regarding the sharing of the auctioned licenses among them before the auction prices get too high.
- *Predatory bids:* These are bids placed by a bidder against a rival at some license that is of high value to that rival but useless to the bidder who submits the predatory bid. The idea is to keep punishing the rival bidder as long as he does not allow the predatory bidder to be standing bidder at one of the rival's licenses.
- *Retaliatory bids:* This type of bids is placed against a bidder who just displaced the standing bidder of a license, by the former standing bidder of that license. This kind of bids is used to signal to the rival that he will be punished if he insists on competing for that license he just claimed.
- *Temporary bids:* These are bids that ensure that the bidder's activity is met so that his eligibility is not reduced in the auction. The bidder places temporary bids for licenses that are of zero value to him so that the prices for the licenses of his interest are not incremented and they

remain hopefully low. Also, these licenses must exhibit some competition so that the bidder is not "accidentally" finally allocated this licenses, thus forcing him to withdraw and pay the penalty fee.

CONCLUSION

This chapter has presented the Simultaneous Multiple Round auction, commonly referred to as the FCC auction, which was used in the United States of America for the allocation of spectrum licenses to wireless telecom providers. The main design decisions have been presented and some related results from auction theory that affected the final design have been provided. As part of this discussion, some additional results of auction theory regarding multi-object auctions have been presented. The FCC auction applications and some indicative auction instances have also been presented, as well as an identification of the main types of bids and strategies observed.

Overall the Simultaneous Multiple Round auction has been considered as a big success both in terms of revenue and efficiency of the spectrum allocation. In most auctions conducted this way, the revenue attained was high and there was an almost uniform spectrum unit price derived by the outcome of the auction; that is, the value of 1MHz of spectrum per person was more or less the same over different regions and bands auctioned simultaneously. The exposure problem did not appear and there were no complaints regarding the transparency of the auction. This huge success motivated the adoption of this auction format by most European countries for conducting the European 3G spectrum auctions. The success of these auctions was more controversial, as discussed in the next chapter.

REFERENCES

[1]   URL:http://wireless.fcc.gov/auctions/default.htm?job=about_auctionsan dpage=2

[2]   Milgrom, P. Putting Auction Theory to Work: The Simultaneous Ascending Auction, *Journal of Political Economy*, 108:2, 245-272, 2000.

[3]   Federal Communications Committee of the USA, Wireless Telecommunications Bureau, URL: http://www.fcc.gov/wtb/auctions/.

[4]   Branco, F. On the Superiority of the Multiple Round Ascending Bid
        Auction, *Economics Letters*, 70, 187-194, 2001.

[5]   Cramton, P. Money Out of Thin Air: The Nationwide Narrowband PCS
        Auction, *Journal of Economics and Management Strategy*, 6:3, 431-
        495, 1995.

[6]   McAfee, P.; McMillan, J. Analyzing the Airwaves Auction, *Journal of
        Economic Perspectives*, 10:1, 159-175, 1996.

[7]   URL:http://wireless.fcc.gov/auctions/default.htm?job=about_auctionsan
        dpage=3

[8]   Ausubel L.; Cramton, P.; McAfee, P.; McMillan, J., Synergies in
        Wireless Telephony: Evidence from the Broadband PCS Auctions,
        Journal of Economics and Management Strategy, 6:3, 497-527, 1997.

[9]   Ausubel L.; Milgrom P. Ascending Auctions with Package Bidding,
        Frontiers of Theoretical Economics, 1:1, 1-44, 2002.

[10]   Charles Rivers Associates Report No 1351-00, Report 1B: Package
        Bidding for Spectrum Licenses, Submitted to the FCC, URL:
        http://www.cramton.umd.edu/papers1995-1999/97/

[11]   Cramton, P.; Mc Millan, J.; Milgrom, P.; Miller, B.; Mitchell, B.,
        Vincent, D.; Wilson, R. Auction Design Enhancements for Non-
        Combinatorial Auctions, Report to the Federal Communications
        Commission, 1997.

[12]   McMillan, J. Why auction the spectrum?, *Telecommunications Policy*,
        19, 191-199, 1995.

[13]   McAfee, P.; McMillan, J. Analyzing the Airwaves Auction, *Journal of
        Economic Perspectives*, 10:1, 159-175, 1996.

[14]   FCC Auction Spectrum Data, URL: http://capcp.psu.edu/FCC/

[15]   URL:http://wireless.fcc.gov/auctions/default.htm?job=auction_summary
        andid=1

[16]   URL: http://wireless.fcc.gov/auctions/04/releases/pnwl5028.pdf

Chapter 5

THE EUROPEAN 3G SPECTRUM AUCTIONS

ABSTRACT

This chapter presents the 3G spectrum auctions, which were conducted in the European Union member countries for the allocation of spectrum licenses to wireless telecom providers. This chapter can be seen as complementary to the previous one, which focused on the applications of the FCC-type auctions in the United States of America. As part of this discussion, this chapter provides a broad coverage of these auctions for which several aspects such as the time instance when they were conducted is of prominent importance. This chapter also provides an analysis of the strategies followed by both the regulators in terms of selecting the auction format and number of licenses and the bidders, i.e. the European telecom providers. Finally, some concluding remarks are provided.

INTRODUCTION

This chapter provides an overview of the European spectrum auctions. These auctions were greatly "inspired" by the auction-based licensing procedure used in the USA, which has already been presented in the previous chapter. As opposed to the USA where the regulator can impose a certain scheme over a wide geographical region, which allows him to define geographical licenses of different size but of equal value, this is not the case in Europe. The European Union is a union of independent states, each of which has ownership of the spectrum within its national borders and can choose the most preferred way of allocating this scarce resource. It is no surprise, that the spectrum allocation procedure for 3G services was diverse in Europe.

A detailed presentation of the inherent features of each auction that determined its success (design decisions, timing, attractiveness and maturity of the market) has already received considerable attention in the literature. This chapter provides an overview, summarizes the main findings, addresses the crucial aspects and provides to the reader some interesting references from where additional material can be obtained.

THE EUROPEAN SPECTRUM AUCTIONS

As already stated previously in the introduction of this chapter, the various European countries opted for generally different spectrum licensing procedures for different number of licences. Moreover, the definition of these licenses, i.e. what frequencies and how much spectrum each license contains, as well as the point in time where these licenses were awarded to the telecom operators also varied a lot. In fact, this was one of the most crucial factors of the licensing procedure that had a great impact on its success or failure.

Table 4.1. The 3G licenses allocation mechanism for the European Union countries (time period: 1999-2002)

Beauty Contest	Auction
Finland	Austria
France	Belgium
Ireland	Denmark
Luxemburg	Germany
Portugal	Greece
Spain	Italy
Sweden	Netherlands
	United Kingdom

The license award procedure was conducted between 1999 and 2002 in most European countries. Not all of them opted to auction the licenses defined. In fact, roughly half of the 15 member states (of that time) of the European Union chose to perform a beauty contest, rather than an auction mechanism of some kind. In both cases the primary goal of the regulator was the economic efficiency, i.e. awarding the spectrum to the companies who could make the best use of it in order to enrich their service offerings for the benefit of the telecom industry and the customers.

The first primary decision of the regulator in all these countries was the *number of licenses* to be awarded. This decision would greatly affect the performance of the award procedure, especially in the case of auctions, since the price in this case depends on the competition: Awarding more licenses increases the supply, thus driving prices down. On the other hand, if it is feasible to offer more licenses, i.e. if there is actual demand for them, this can result in attracting more players in the local telecom market, thus increasing competition in the long-term. The latter is expected to produce more choices for the customers and better value for money for the services offered.

Beauty contests are less transparent and they have attracted much criticism since this means of allocation both a priori and a posteriori, as observed in practise in the various European 3G beauty contests, favour incumbents and result in entry deterrence for new players in the market. In the remainder of this chapter, we henceforth restrict attention to the European 3G auctions.

The rule that was adopted by almost all European countries was that the number of 3G licenses would be equal to that of the GSM operators already active in the national market plus one. An exception to this rule was Luxembourg that offered two additional licenses compared to the number of the 2G national operators.

A surprising bad decision of the Netherlands was to award a number of 3G licenses equal to that of the 2G operators (i.e. five): this clearly signaled to potential new entrants that they had limited chance of being awarded a license. This was evident in the Netherlands auction where new entrants chose to create coalitions with local 2G operators rather than compete against them in the auction, leading the auction to a fiasco.

Finally, Austria and Germany decided to auction a certain number of frequency blocks allowing for bidders to bid for either 2 or 3 of them in order to combine them to form a single license; market would shape the number of licenses offered via the auction procedure.

Overall, offering additional licenses (or frequency blocks) was a direct attempt of the national regulatory authorities in Europe to attract new players in the market that could make use of the additional license.

This was also the case for countries where due to the budget constraints of the telecom operators and the inherent features/problems of each country regarding the financial status or the geographical isolation with the rest of EU attracting more competitors in the market was already considered to be very difficult; then, typically additional incentives for market entry were given in order to invite participation in the auction. A prominent case is Greece, which at the time of the auction had no terrestrial borders with any other EU country. This, along with the generally lower than average income of the population, and thus the potential profitability of 3G services, combined with the higher cost of deploying a network due to the rough terrain and the large number of islands, clearly limited the attractiveness of the country's licenses. In order to cope with this hurdle, Greece adopted a pay-your-bid auction procedure with high reserve prices for the licenses: however the reserve price would be lower in case a new entrant would bid for a license. Though this design was sound, it proved of limited value in practice due to the economic circumstances of the time, which prohibited any other company (with the exception of the three 2G incumbents) to bid for additional 3G spectrum licenses.

Regarding the amount of spectrum that was made available for each license, the majority for the countries opted for a "uniform" definition, i.e. licenses of 2 x 15 MHz (paired spectrum) + 1 x 5 MHz (unpaired spectrum). This definition was adopted by Belgium, Denmark, Finland, France, Ireland, Luxemburg, Portugal, Spain and Sweden. This was a conscious decision of these countries to allow for a uniform definition of the licenses auctioned so as to be more attractive for the big European operators that could bid in multiple countries in order to combine them and build multi-national aggregates of licenses over neighboring EU countries. The exact amount of the spectrum offered was also in line with the 3G technology technical considerations. Geographically isolated countries typically deviated from this rule for multiple reasons. For instance, the UK due to the high both expected a priori and actual (observed) competition in the auction, defined multiple license sizes. Hence, it adopted a smart design decision and used spectrum as a means of differentiating the value of each license in order to further promote the competition in the auction.

The expected competition in each auction was only a result of each country's geography, the inherent features of the national economy and how fiscally vibrant its national telecom operators were. The *timeline* of the auctions was a crucial factor as well. The first auction was the UK auction conducted in April 2000. The auction format was similar to that of the FCC, i.e. the simultaneous ascending auctioning of all 5 licenses offered. At that time, the European big operators were in an extremely good fiscal shape and there were large (in fact too optimistic) expectations from the 3G services and their expected profitability. This over-enthusiasm, combined with the large population of the UK greatly favoured the auction: It was a huge success, attaining high revenue for the state after fierce competition of 13 rivals for 5 licenses. This was no coincidence: it was a conscious decision of the UK auction design team to run the auction as soon as possible.

Three months later than the UK auction, the German auction for 3G took place. An interesting peculiarity of this auction was that the regulator decided to auction blocks of spectrum rather than licenses. In particular, 12 blocks were offered. The auction rules allowed for bidders to bid for either 2 or 3 frequency blocks in order to combine them to a single license, thus the auction outcome in terms of the number of licenses to be awarded was unknown a priori. Competition was rather weak, with 7 bidders participating and soon one of them dropped out of the auction leaving 6 bidders to compete for 12 blocks of spectrum. At that point it would be expected that the bidders would perform *demand reduction*, i.e. bid for only two frequency blocks each, and end the auction, since attempting to displace a bidder by bidding aggressively for a third spectrum block would increase significantly the auction prices and reduce the bidders' net benefit.

However, there was a notable exception to this rule: Deutche Telekom irrationally insisted on pursuing the allocation of 3 blocks, driving prices up and preventing the auction from ending. Finally Deutche Telekom accepted the fact that it could win just 2 blocks, but prolonging the auction resulted in very high revenue for the state. The fact that Deutche Telekom is a company owned by the German state – that would greatly benefit from the auction revenue – seems to be the only rational explanation for this "irrational" bidding strategy. The German design did not payoff and the good performance of the auction was mostly due to the bidding behaviour of Deutche Telekom. In fact, the Austrian 3G auction that copied the German 3G auction design ended up in a fiasco, resulting in one sixth of the per-capita revenue raised in Germany [3].

As time elapsed, the expectations of the industry for the value of the 3G licenses were greatly reduced. Also, a stock-market crisis greatly affected the fiscal condition of the few large European operators that could create a pan-European 3G network: since these companies had already been obliged to invest high amounts of money in other national 3G auctions already conducted, the European countries that were among the last to auction their licenses had very limited chances of attracting new entrants in the market and attaining high revenues. This can be seen as a form of the *declining price anomaly* that appears in the sequential auctions (already discussed in a previous chapter of this book). This trend is evident in the European 3G auctions where as time elapses both the revenue (normalized by means of the revenue per capita) and the difference of the number of bidders minus the number of licenses offered decline dramatically.

For instance in the UK auction, which was the first to be conducted, in April 2000, there were 13 bidders for 5 licenses and the revenue attained was 36.1 billion Euro. Similarly, Germany conducted its auction in August 2000: 7 bidders competed for 6 licenses and the attained revenue was 50.1 billion Euros. The subsequent auction in Italy in October 2000 raised 12.2 billion Euros, the result of 6 bidders competing for 5 licenses offered. The auction in Belgium in March 2001, where 4 bidders competed for 3 licenses attained 0.6 billion Euros. The auction in Greece, one of the last to be conducted, took place in July 2001 and there were 3 bidders "competing" for 4 licenses: the resulting 0.5 billion Euros of revenue was a result of the high reserve prices. However, it is clear that the lack of additional bidders had its toll in the performance of these auctions.

The outcome in most European auctions was that the number of 3G licenses auctioned was more than the existing number of 2G licenses. The typical case is that an additional license was both auctioned and awarded to bidders. Prominent exceptions to this rule are Austria and Germany, where two additional licenses, reaching a total of 6 licenses, were acquired (by means of the 12 frequency block auction). Finally, in Greece and Belgium only 3 licenses - out of the 4 offered in the auction - were finally awarded, thus resulting in an equal number of 3G and 2G licenses in these countries.

A detailed presentation of the data for the European 3G auctions can be found in [1], [2], [3], [4] and [5].

Overall, the following factors were the most prominent in determining the outcome of these auctions:

Timing and evolution of market expectations and budgets: The 2G/3G telecom operators' fiscal status, as well as their expectations over the value of the 3G licenses auctions greatly diminished after the September of 2000, crippling competition in subsequent auctions. Budget constraints of big pan-European players greatly affected their budget for auctions that took place after the autumn of 2000, which combined with the lower valuations greatly affected the outcome.

The number of licenses offered: The additional license offered was a clear invitation for the big European operators to bid in the various national auctions in order to create pan-European aggregation of licenses. Offering an excessive number of licenses would not be sustainable by the market, whose potential was already more or less already known due to the presence of a certain number of 2G telecom operators. The (N+1) number of licenses rule adopted (where N is the number of 2G operators already active in each country) proved to be very successful in practise. Offering an equal number of licenses (as in the Netherlands) is a bad design decision resulting in entry deterrence of new players and a fiasco for the auction.

The auction design: The peculiarities of each auction design were of prominent importance. The UK auction adopted an ascending FCC-type auction format due to the fierce competition expected (and realized in the auction). Subsequent auctions relied in sealed-bid formats and high reserve prices for the licenses (e.g. in Greece), so as to mitigate the risk of attaining very low – or even zero – revenue. There is not a general rule that can be applied, since there is a multitude of factors that affects the competition to be exhibited in the various countries and it is also important that the auction rules mitigate collusion and attract bidders.

It is no surprise that European 3G auctions conducted in the year 2000, i.e. the UK auction (April 2000), the Netherlands auction (July 2000), the German auction (July 2000), the Italian auction (October 2000), the Austrian auction (November 2000), the Swiss auction (December 2000) all adopted an ascending format. On the contrary, the remaining 2001 auctions opted for a sealed-bid format and high reserve prices so as to deal with the low market expectations and thus the limited expected competition in the bidding. This approach did pay off, since this format adopted e.g. by Greece succeeded in attaining more than twice the per capita revenue of the much more competitive (taking place in a much richer country of the central Europe) Swiss auction [3].

Bad auction designs can lead to a fiasco, even when the market conditions are more or less good. A typical example of the latter is the Turkish auction [4] where a sequential design was opted, with the selling price of the first license to be used as the reserve price of the second! This surprisingly bad and unjustified decision had its toll in the outcome: The winner of the first auction chose to bid very high so as to prevent the awarding of the second license, rendering him a monopoly in the market! This was a rational decision of the winner, since the revenues of a monopoly are greatly higher than that of a duopoly, thus allowing the high bid on the first license.

Using prior experience and successful auction designs provides some safety, rather than "experimenting" with unjustified auction design decisions. However, it is important to customize each auction format to the specific market conditions and needs, so as to fine-tune it and increase its efficiency. As it is correctly stated in [2], "In auction design, the devil is in the details".

Geography: Geographical and cultural similarity was also a prominent factor. Due to the increased mobility among the neighboring EU countries, the similar language, income and cultural status of neighboring countries in e.g. Central Europe, the licenses of these countries were highly valued by the European operators that aimed to establish a large geographical footprint. In fact, this has motivated some economists [5] to propose that it is worthwhile considering some kind of "European super-auction" that allows a continental (or EU) aggregation of spectrum, in addition to the various national licenses.

CONCLUSION

The European 3G auctions were greatly affected by both the market conditions/expectations for the 3G services and the design decisions. The timeline turned out to be a key factor as well, since the last auctions were conducted in a very negative environment with few interested bidders that were extremely budget-constrained. Most European countries tried to adopt the auction design to the market needs and conditions expected in each country. This chapter provided specific examples where good auction design decisions led to a decent outcome, even under bad conditions, and also commented on the negative impact of bad design decisions.

The impact of the auctioning of the 3G licenses in the wireless telecom operators is also a controversial issue: Supporters of auctions claim that efficiency and revenue are important goals in the allocation of the scarce radio spectrum and auctions have proven their worth in achieving both. On the contrary, beauty contests lack transparency and deter market entry. The criticism of the auctions comes mostly from the companies that were forced to bid very highly for those licenses: they perceive auctions as a means of taxation and an additional cost that will be a potential obstacle to the fast deployment of the 3G networks and services. However, this is not fully supported by the data. For instance, Finland decided to allocate 3G licenses by means of a beauty contest for free – actually operators pay a yearly fee of 1000 Euros per 25 KHz, thus 0.2 million Euros for 5 MHz, which is considered a negligible amount of money – as opposed to Germany where the auction revenue were considerably high (second highest per capita revenue in EU). However, the rollout of 3G networks and services in Finland is far behind from that of Germany, leading many analysts to claim that the high license acquisition costs are actually motivating companies to deploy networks and services as soon as possible in order to be compensated for their investments.

Concluding, it is worth emphasizing that careful auction design clearly proved its worth in the case of the European 3G auctions and useful lessons were learned about how to run such auctions. Bidders also learned the value of careful valuation estimation, rational bidding and avoiding winner's curse. Regulators succeeded in awarding efficiently the spectrum available to an increased number of players in the market (compared to those active in 2G) and attaining total revenue of 109 billion Euros for the European member states. The potential of a pan-European auction is an interesting research proposal that is worth investigating; however, there are important obstacles that need to be overcomed due to the fragmented nature of Europe where multiple independent countries own the radio spectrum.

REFERENCES

[1]   McKinsey Final Report for the European Commission. Comparative Assessment of the Licensing Regimes for 3G Mobile Communications in the European Union and their Impact on the Mobile Communications Sector, June 25, 2002. URL: http://ec.europa.eu/information_society/ topics/telecoms/radiospec/doc/pdf/mobiles/mckinsey_study/final_report .pdf

[2]   Klemperer, P. What Really Matters in Auction Design. *The Journal of Economic Perspectives*, 16:1, pp. 169-189, 2002.

[3]   Klemperer, P. How (not) to run auctions: The European 3G Telecom Auctions. *European Economic Review*, 46:4-5, pp. 829-845, 2002

[4]   Binmore, K.; Klemperer, P. The Biggest Auction Ever: The Sale of the British 3G Telecom Licenses. *The Economic Journal*, 112:478, pp. 74-96, 2002.

[5]   Jehiel, P.; Moldovanu, B. The European UMTS/IMT-2000 License Auctions. Working Paper, Univ. of Mannheim, 2001. URL: http://ideas. repec.org/p/xrs/sfbmaa/01-20.html

Chapter 6

AUCTIONS AND ELECTRONIC MARKETS

ABSTRACT

This chapter presents the use of auctions in telecoms-related electronic markets. A discussion of the presence of auctions in various kinds of marketplaces and electronic systems is briefly discussed for completeness reasons. The main features of the auctions adopted for electronic markets are briefly mentioned. Their differences with respective to the classical definition of those mechanisms are highlighted and intuitively explained. Subsequently, this chapter focuses on the use of auctions in electronic markets that are used by telecom providers for the lease of telecommunication assets. Finally, an indicative auction design that could be adopted for a telecom spectrum market and a comprehensive execution example of this auction are presented.

AUCTIONS AND INTERNET ELECTRONIC MARKETS

Commercial sites that host user-initiated auctions, such as *Ebay* [1] perform transactions of many millions of dollars on a daily basis. The vast majority of the existing e-marketplaces (including eBay) support solely simple, i.e. single-object auctions. This implies that the auctioning of multiple similar items can be done either by means of auctioning them together (as a single bundle), which means that only one winner will be awarded all the items – too restrictive for most practical cases – or by means of un-correlated independent auctions. For example, under the eBay approach, an owner of 5 identical items typically organizes 5 separate auctions or auctions all the items together as one lot; the users interested in 2 or more items would have to bid in multiple auctions.

Hence, significant logistic overheads are incurred and the whole trading process is somehow complicated in this case. The motivation behind this is the simplicity of the single-unit auctions and the fact that most users simply auction just one item.

Regarding the support of single-object auctions, the existing e-market-places support more or less the same popular mechanisms. These are the simple English and sealed-bid auction formats presented in Chapter 2, with an important modification: The termination point of the English auction is not determined by the bidding activity but is set *a priori* by the seller. Thus, all the auction participants *a priori* know the precise instance in time where the auction's bidding phase will have been completed. This greatly affects users' strategies, since bidders can remain silent throughout the auction procedure so as to keep the current standing price low and then submit a high bid towards the closing time of the auction. Needless to say, under this format the information conveyed to the bidders throughout the bidding phase is of typically limited value and use, as opposed to the format of the simple auctions that follows the rules presented in the Chapter 2. The most widely used auction format in such e-marketplaces is the English auction format - with the aforementioned modification of the fixed termination point in time.

Note also that the presence of bidding agents for simple English auctions that are constituent part of the aforementioned e-marketplaces is limited. Recently, eBay has offered to its users a bidding agent for its simple English auctions; its strategy is rather simple, i.e. the agent tops a rival bid as long as the former is submitted and provided that the submission of the new bid is allowed by the user's budget constraints. The main argument for the lack of bidding agents is that users do not trust agents and refuse to use them in practice. They prefer to manually bid towards the closing time of the auction *(sniping)*, thus raising concerns on the use of agents. This is an indication that indeed users do not trust the strategy of the eBay agent as opposed to all agents in general. This is simply because the strategy of these agents is considered by users as more beneficial for the seller and due to the limited control that users have over the agents' behavior. This is also why the same users prefer to use other commercial bidding agents to bid on their behalf in eBay auctions. Indeed, there is a variety of commercial bidding agents for eBay auctions which perform sniping.

The eBay's bidding agent has a fixed strategy, which is to place a new bid whenever a rival tops his own bid. The user just declares his willingness to pay and has no other way to influence the agent's behavior. Since multiple instances of this agent may represent multiple users and compete against each other in the same auction, it is clear that this agent's strategy drives prices up and limits the winner's profits.

Finally, it is worth mentioning that *electricity* is typically traded by a complex auction-based market system. In particular, the typical market comprises of conducting a yearly and monthly auction for per-year and per-month long-term contracts for supplying electricity to the system, i.e. the grid. In order to accommodate demand spikes on daily basis, additional auctions are performed. Also demand spikes are taken into account by computing spot prices and activating supply within a 10 minutes duration time scale.

Additional markets that use auctions are the markets used by industries in order to purchase the right to emit certain quantities of carbon dioxide and greenhouse gasses in general. Auctions are also typically used in selling wine, flowers, fish, air tickets, all kinds of equipment, real estate properties, diamonds and crude oil. Since these markets are not related to telecoms, we refrain from providing additional information in this book. In addition to the discussion and references already provided in Chapters 2 and 3, supplementary information and a nice presentation of these applications of auctions can be found by the interested reader in [2], [3].

TELECOM-RELATED AUCTION-BASED MARKETS

The use of auctions in various fields of e-commerce has also its applications in telecoms-related markets. The most prominent case is that of bandwidth exchanges. In particular, special markets called bandwidth markets (or exchanges) offer a large number of point-to-point circuits of certain capacity. Some of these bandwidth exchanges, such as Arbinet [4] and eSwitch [5] focus on real-time aggregation and matching of supply and demand for call-minutes in spot markets. Liquid bandwidth exchanges offer real time trading of bandwidth for time scales as small as 5 minutes and allow the buyers to purchase bandwidth from any available seller, without binding contracts [6]. An extensive list and description of bandwidth markets can be found in [7].

Moreover, vendors of network equipment such as Cisco sell a wide variety of routers that enable the multiplexing of thousands of simultaneous Virtual Private Networks (VPNs) or private circuit sessions. Note also that this functionality can be further enhanced by advanced Traffic Engineering software that implements the virtual router (VR) concept [8]. Thus, it is feasible for the network providers nowadays to implement in their network advanced resource allocation policies of the finest granularity. Also, utilities - such as electricity companies - that have telecommunications networks and services are expected to offer part of their networks' capacity for sale to bandwidth markets.

This trend has also recently resulted in specialized bandwidth markets for wireless spectrum, called "spectrum exchanges". The idea behind this kind of markets is to bring together the wireless telecom operators who specialize in operating a wide variety of networks, from narrowband to broadband PCS and 2G+ cellular networks. Owners of spectrum can auction an entire license, comprising of a multitude of frequencies within a certain frequency band, as a single item, or auction the frequency carriers separately. Buyers may buy the auctioned good or "lease" it, i.e. buy the right to use it for their own network for a given amount of time. Currently, to the author's knowledge, there is one commercial spectrum exchange, namely SpecEx [9]. SpecEx is estimated to have a repository of spectrum whose value is approximately $250 million.

Though SpecEx is the only official spectrum exchange market, there are also "informal" secondary markets in the United States. This means that wireless operators trade among them slices of spectrum without having created an official marketplace. To be more precise, vast companies such as Verizon Wireless and Sprint Nextel Corp. frequently purchase small slices of spectrum from other smaller companies and institutions owning spectrum, such as universities, the church and local area wireless providers. The resulting transfers of ownership are routinely approved by the FCC.

It is worth emphasizing that the dynamic spectrum exchange comprises a business opportunity for new entrants in the wireless services market. Indeed, there are cases where startup wireless Internet Service Providers such as Clearwire Corp., have been built exclusively by purchasing chunks of spectrum by means of such business transactions. Public-safety agencies are also active buyers in the secondary market.

This practice of leasing part of the spectrum of an underutilized wireless service provider in order for another company to serve its customers is not solely a USA market phenomenon. The same trend also appears in the European wireless markets, where owners of licensed spectrum accommodate the needs of smaller providers by means of either short-term or long-term leasing of part of their spectrum.

Regulatory authorities in many European countries, New Zealand and Australia, use secondary spectrum trading. Activity in these markets has generally been very limited, with the exception of Australia where trading has been more active. The Australian Communications and Media Authority (ACMA) [10] is Australia's regulator for broadcasting, the Internet, radio communications and telecommunications. It is responsible for approving all secondary license trading and collects and publishes the related data.

A detailed reporting, as well as a full description of the trading rules can be found in [11]. Below, we provide some indicative data, which demonstrates the activity with secondary market license trading:

Table 6.1. Trading in licenses in Australia since 2004 [11]

License	Transfers				
	01/01/04 to 30/06/04	2004-05	2005-06	2006-07	2007-08
Point to point	171	296	207	377	149
Point to multipoint	69	61	37	92	55
Land mobile system	615	497	731	649	694
Ambulatory	57	192	132	73	228
Paging system	8	32	29	27	19
Broadcasting service	6	152	302	17	143
Narrowband Area Service	10	15	49	64	7
Narrowcasting Service	79	127	54	80	114
Total licenses transferred	1284	1794	1948	1628	1685

This increasingly dynamic nature of the market is further enhanced by the Software Defined Radio (SDR) technology. In particular, SDR allows the possibility of reconfiguring a particular Base Station (BS) to WLAN Office system during the day and wide area for busy hour or 2G to 3G or vice-versa depending upon the nature of the traffic [12]. Several business models are analyzed in [12] and the various business opportunities for the telecom operators by adopting this technology are reported. For instance, the SDR approach also applies to Network Rollout where 3G Services can be dynamically rolled out to areas using 2/2.5G infrastructure according to customer demand. Moreover, handsets manufacturers benefit from economies of scale in the construction of SDR-enabled handsets. Note also that due to the dynamic reuse of the spectrum the latter can be (re-)used more efficiently.

This new concept of dynamically reconfigurable spectrum also makes both feasible and plausible to dynamically lease the spectrum by means of auction mechanisms in secondary markets. Finally, this implies that virtual network operators, leasing chunks of spectrum of existing wireless operator, could provide services to their customers by dynamically bidding for as much spectrum they really need in these markets. Therefore, the wireless spectrum market is far from static, despite the licensing procedure adopted for leasing chunks of spectrum, which has also been presented in the previous two chapters of this book.

No surprise SDR and secondary spectrum markets where spectrum is dynamically reallocated by means of auctions have received considerable attention. Regulatory authorities and wireless telecom operators in USA, Europe and Australia agree that secondary markets are beneficial and can provide a useful means of efficiently utilizing the spectrum available and promoting competition in the industry, thus resulting in better, more sophisticated telecom services for the consumers who are offered by the wireless telecom providers in low prices.

In the United Kingdom, Ofcom estimates that spectrum trading in secondary markets will result in net economic benefits between GBP 67 million to GBP 144 million if the impact of increased competition is taken into account. Moreover, DotEcon and Hogan and Hartson estimated that benefits resulting from the additional competition that would result from spectrum trading to be around GBP 154 million. This report also emphasizes on the network effects and the additional benefits that the intensification of the competition will bring [13].

In order to clarify how these developments are associated with auctions, we proceed to define an auction mechanism that is well fitted in this dynamic context.

A SPECTRUM EXCHANGE SAMPLE AUCTION DESIGN

As explained in the previous section, there is an increasing interest in the creation of marketplaces that aggregate idle spectrum of wireless infrastructure-based networks (classified per technology type) belonging to several telecom companies in order to auction them periodically. This section discusses the various requirements that should be met by an auction design for such a spectrum auction under the assumption of competition for the idle spectrum.

This assumption is motivated by the fixed quantity of the spectrum available per communication network technology combined with the increasing popularity of data services. As explained in the remainder of this section, these have motivated our choice of a multi-unit sealed-bid auction. Note that such a design is also in accordance with what has been adopted to most existing spectrum marketplaces, though the auction proposed here does not claim to match any of the existing adopted schemes.

Auction Model and Objectives

We assume that there are $q(t)$ idle frequency bands capable of serving a certain type of network technology, i.e. frequency bands of a certain range. Our model prescribes that such identical frequency bands are auctioned *simultaneously* at time epoch t. It is also assumed that the winners of the auction lease those resources for the same predefined time period, i.e. the results of the auction all apply for the same time interval.

Both the supply and demand for resources is discretized in integral units, pertaining to the number of MHz for each license's type. To keep the presentation simple, we refrain from repeating throughout the section that all the frequency bands are identical in the sense that are of the same type and that multiple instances of the spectrum auction, one per frequency band type are held simultaneously. Instead, we use the term "spectrum auction" to refer to anyone of those instances. It is also worth noting that the number of instances of the spectrum auction that are to be run simultaneously depends on the variety of the network technologies and the respective frequency bands that are adequate to serve them, but also depends on the various leasing periods supported. The latter means that different markets for short-term and long-term reservations for the same type of spectrum frequency bands could be co-existing.

The constraints and objectives regarding the mechanism sought are:

- Bidders should be allowed to submit multiple bids, denoting the desired per-unit willingness to pay for a certain quantity of units. These bids are complementary rather than substitutes; that is, they do not represent alternative preferences but when put together express the entire demand function of the bidder.
- In general, bids should be fully satisfied. This means that each bidder should be able to reserve the exact quantity – or in general one of the

desired quantities requested by means of a set of bids – of wireless spectrum he is bidding for, or none. This applies to all the bids since allocating fractions of the users' demand may be worthless to the competing wireless telecom providers, who need a certain quantity of bandwidth in order to accommodate their needs. On the other hand and in order to keep the mechanism simple and ensure the liquidity of the market, we do not allow for users to denote as part of their bid that they accept their bid to be partially satisfied, i.e. allocate to the respective bid a smaller quantity of units that those requested.

- The mechanism should be practically applicable. This implies that the mechanism should be i) *scalable* with respect to both the number of units auctioned and the number of users and ii) *reliable, transparent* and *not susceptible to dishonest dealing*. This is of extreme importance so as to ensure that wireless telecom providers would be interested in participating in the auction.

- The overhead of the auction should be minimal; the number of messages to be exchanged among sellers and buyers should be kept small and the respective computation should be performed fast. The latter ensures that the auction can be run periodically for small time periods, thus accommodating consumers' demand spikes for computation. This is an attractive feature that combined with the co-existence of short-term and long-term markets makes the particular mechanism design highly flexible and attractive for the wireless telecom providers.

- The mechanism should be able to simultaneously auction units that belong to different owners (telecom providers) who want to offer at the market some (idle) resources that they have leased and are currently under-utilized. In both these cases, it is required that the determination of the units sold and the respective "sharing" of the revenue attained – even in cases where supply exceeds demand – to the respective owners of the units in a both fair and generally acceptable way be feasible.

Note also that it is likely that the telecom providers bidding for spectrum at the spectrum auction have also long-term contracts with certain wireless providers. In, fact, one may envision virtual wireless service providers who do not actually own wireless assets infrastructure but lease it by means of contracts and bidding in such a market.

For such customers, it is very likely that it is considered desirable for them to prefer to be allocated at the auction units that belong to the same provider whom they have already committed to. This way, they can ensure that they are allocated adjacent frequency bands, thus giving them the opportunity to utilize the guard band of these bands. The guard band is the portion of the wireless band that is not used so that there is no interference among different networks; obviously, if adjacent bands belong to the same wireless telecom provider this spectrum can be used to serve customers while interference is no longer an issue. This final additional user-imposed constraint is also one that should be accommodated by the spectrum auction.

Why Combinatorial Approaches Are Inapplicable

The requirement that each bidder should be able to reserve the exact quantity of units he is bidding for, combined with the fact that each user may have a preferred provider, seems to motivate the choice of a combinatorial mechanism.

In a combinatorial auction of M items each bidder is allowed to place a bid $b_i(S) > 0$ for any combination (bundle) of distinct items (i.e. frequency bands) S which is subset of M. However, winner determination in this case is in general NP-hard, thus it is computationally intractable for practical cases. Therefore, this approach is inapplicable for real-world markets comprising of large number of participants and goods.

Clearly, this indicates that the spectrum auction is to be implemented in a multi-unit non-combinatorial fashion, allowing users to submit multiple additive bids for various quantities of items but forbidding combinatorial bids.

Why Progressive/Ascending Auctions Are Inapplicable

Progressive auctions prescribe that the auction is conducted in a (typically unknown a priori) number of rounds. There are multiple mechanisms and variations, but the typical form of a progressive auction is as follows: Price is initially low and bidders gradually improve their bids as the price ascends, or alternatively by replying to rivals' bids. Improvement of bids means that subsequent bids of the same bidder should be increasing in the per-unit price offered for the demanded quantity of spectrum and also non-increasing in the quantity of spectrum. Thus, as time elapses, the aggregate demand for the monotonically increasing market price is gradually reduced and at some time in time it eventually matches the aggregate supply. At this point, the auction is considered to have ended and the standing bidders are awarded the units auctioned.

As the aforementioned presentation of this class of auction mechanisms indicates, the main problem of these mechanisms is their complexity. Ascending auctions require a possibly large time to terminate and they rely on the exchange of a big number of messages and feedback. The overhead of this procedure, as well as the overhead of the processing of all those messages in order for the providers to follow a certain strategy renders this class of auction mechanisms complicated.

The synchronization of the users in rounds is non-trivial due to the different delays that users may experience over the network. The need for complex techniques such as time-stamping of the messages exchanged increase the overhead of the mechanism and the complexity of the respective implementation of the auction. Also, even if proxy bidding is adopted to mitigate this issue, the resulting overhead in resources for the auction increases significantly.

Moreover, the fact that this type of auctions fails to provide an *a priori known* completion time is also an undesirable feature. On the contrary, sealed auctions do not suffer from these problems and can also produce higher revenue even in cases where the level of competition is not very high. Furthermore, sealed-bid mechanisms perform better than ascending auctions in case of *ex ante asymmetries* among bidders. Indeed, the latter seems to be the typical case for the wireless telecommunication market where few large and smaller providers co-exist [14].

On the other hand, ascending auctions are known to reduce winners' curse and are considered to promote competition, under the assumption that the goods auctioned are of common value. Overall, neither theory nor empirical studies conclude that there is in general a superior format [14].

Thus a sealed auction design is opted, mostly for simplicity reasons and this format's satisfactory performance in terms of revenue in cases of low competition.

Outline of the Winner Determination Rule

So far, we have motivated our choice of a multi-unit sealed-bid auction. Therefore, users submit multi-unit bids, these are ranked at the winner determination phase and the highest bids (in terms of the denoted willingness to pay) are declared as winning. We need to complement our mechanism with a payment rule that prescribes what winners pay for the units allocated.

The Payment Rule

There are three possible choices for the payment rule: i) Vickrey ii) Uniform and iii) Pay-your-bid. We discuss on the pros and cons of these payment rules below:

A Vickrey-type payment rule prescribes that each user is charged according to the social opportunity cost that his presence entails. This means that each bidder is charged for the kth object he wins with the kth highest losing bid, submitted by another bidder. Hence, each user pays for the units he is awarded the losing bids that would have become winning if all his own bids were set to zero. Hence, winners pay less than their respective bids. This rule's main merit is that it provides proper incentives for bidders to be truth telling, thus maximizing the social welfare attained. However, despite this theoretical advantage, there are several problems that mitigate its practical applicability:

First of all, under this mechanism it is possible for a dishonest auctioneer to cheat on the bidders by injecting phantom bids in the auction: This way much of the bidders' surplus can be transferred to the provider, thus rendering the mechanism non-transparent and unreliable for the market. The fear of this possibility may affect users' bidding strategy in practice, mitigating this auction's main merit.

Each winner's charge is in general different: In fact, it is likely that two users may end up with different charges, even if the total quantity of units allocated to them is the same. The bidders could perceive this as unfair. Also, this may be in conflict with telecommunications laws in certain countries that prescribe that similar telecom assets should not be priced differently.

The payment rule results in higher computational complexity, since a per-winner charge must be computed and is often regarded as non-intuitive for bidders.

The uniform payment rule prescribes that all winners pay the same price, namely the price of the point where the aggregate demand curve crosses the aggregate supply curve. In practice, this means that all users are charged with the lowest winning or alternatively the highest losing bid. This payment rule provides the users the incentive to be truth telling only under the assumption of bidders' single-unit demand.

In case of multi-unit demand though, which is also the typical case for the Grid marketplace, this payment rule suffers from *demand reduction* [14]: Bidders submit a different demand curve than their real, demanding at every price less quantity than the one that the "honest" demand curve dictates. This strategy aims in keeping prices low and gaining higher payoff for fewer units of good. This strategy mitigates both the providers' revenues and the value of the social welfare attained. Last but not least, a dishonest auctioneer may affect the cutoff price by injecting *phantom bids*, so that the cutoff price that will be paid by the users for all the units awarded to them is substantially increased.

The pay-your-bid payment rule is clearly the simplest one: Each user pays for each unit awarded to him his respective winning bid. Therefore, there is no uncertainty regarding user's final charge if his bid is to become winning.

Obviously, under the pay-your-bid payment rule users will shade their bids in order to attain some discount, i.e. they will not report their valuations truthfully by means of their bids. However, this bid shading is expected to be small if there will be a large number of small competing users in the marketplace, since in that case of competition the market's participants can be regarded essentially as price-takers.

Moreover, the sealed-bid format of the auction increases the bidders' risk of submitting low bids, since in addition to the obvious fact that a low bid has limited probability of being winning, is it also that bidders cannot coordinate and perform signaling by means of their bids so as to share the auctioned goods amongst them under low prices, as opposed to progressive mechanisms. Last but not least, the users' final charge cannot be affected by the injection of phantom bids by the seller, as is the case for both the Vickrey and the uniform payment rule.

Concluding, we have opted for a pay-your-bid payment rule.

REVENUE SHARING RULE

In this subsection we discuss the issue of revenue sharing on distributed versus centralized spectrum markets and complete the mechanism design of the previous subsection. In particular, it is worth noting that in a combinatorial auction design it is impossible to determine how the revenue for a combination of spectrum goods, obtained due to a user's combinatorial bid, should be split among the wireless operators offering this spectrum in the market.

The auction determines the leasing of the computational elements of multiple wireless telecom providers. This is actually an attractive feature since the larger the market, the higher its liquidity is and the more competitive it is. But this fact also implies that a revenue sharing rule is needed to specify which of the units auctioned are to be allocated to winners and what each provider's attained revenue is. Defining the former is trivial in case demand exceeds supply: All units are allocated to the highest bids, provided that these exceed the auction's reserve price (if any). On the other hand, the total revenue collected is shared fairly among providers as follows (this is actually a proportional fairness rationale, though there are alternative ways to do that):

$$revenue(Provider\_i) = total\_revenue * units\_sold(Provider\_i) / total\_units\_sold,$$

In this case, the number of units sold by each provider (reps. totally) equals the number of units offered by the provider (resp. in total).

Note that these rules encourage and reward the wireless telecom providers' participation in the spectrum auction. Also, they provide a fair means of sharing the revenue attained among the providers, without resorting to complex and ambiguous rules, such as the round-robin allocation of high and low bids to the providers for purposes of balancing the revenues in a fair way. Also, this way though we enforce price discrimination for bidders, the same does not apply for providers, all of which sell each of their units at a uniform price, namely the average price. This is also important since the regulatory laws of telecommunication in many countries prohibit the sale of similar telecom assets under differentiated pricing. Last but not least, this rule is both simple and computationally fast.

Finally, the units to be awarded as well as the attained revenue are shared proportionally among the providers. That is:

$$units\_sold(Provider\_i) = total\_units\_sold * units\_offered(Provider\_i) / total\_units\_offered$$

$$revenue(Provider\_i) = total\_revenue * units\_sold(Provider\_i) / total\_units\_sold,$$

Two last observations are in order. First, note that the above rule for distributing the revenue in case of low demand gives providers the incentive to make available as many resource units as possible, in order to sell a larger portion of the quantity totally sold. This is a desirable incentive. Furthermore, note that we have implicitly assumed that the reserve price, if actually non-zero, is the same for all providers participating in the same instance of the auction. We have opted for this, rather than allowing for each provider to set his own reserve price, because this would complicate the winner determination phase. Moreover, if the various reserve prices were to be taken into account in the revenue sharing phase, then, similarly to a double auction, this would create incentives for providers to fluctuate their reserve prices in order to benefit; this effect is not desirable.

SPECTRUM AUCTION EXECUTION EXAMPLE

We present below a comprehensive example of the execution of an instance of the proposed spectrum auction.

First, let us assume that there are in general three providers of resources, namely P1, P2 and P3, offering 25, 35 and 40 units of resources (i.e. frequency chunks) respectively for the current instance of the spectrum auction. Therefore, the total supply of resources is 100 units.

Bidders place their (sealed) bids within the pre-specified bidding period and subsequently the winner determination is performed. In our example, there are six bidders participating in the auction, namely B1, B2, B3, B4, B5 and B6. Table 6.2 depicts the bids submitted.

Table 6.2. The spectrum auction bids

Bidder	Quantity (units)	Per-unit Price (€)
B1	10	7
B1	5	5
B2	20	8
B3	20	9
B3	10	3
B4	10	9
B4	5	6
B5	20	8
B6	15	8

Note that in practice, it is expected that a large number of bidders would be participating in the auction, each demanding a small portion of the total supply of resources. However, in our example the bidders' number is small and their respective demand for resources is significant, in order to simplify the presentation.

After the reception of all bids, these are ordered with respect to the per-unit price, so that winner determination is performed. The sorted bids are depicted as Table 6.3.

Table 6.3. The spectrum auction bids sorted

Bidder	Quantity (units)	Per-unit Price (€)
B4	10	9
B3	20	9
B2	20	8
B6	15	8
B5	20	8
B1	10	7
B4	5	6
B1	5	5
B3	10	3

After the bids are sorted, the 7 highest bids are declared as winning. Note that since the total supply of resources is 100 units, the second bid of B4 is the cut-off point for the auction, i.e. the auction cutoff bid. Subsequently, the auction allocates the specific units to the auction winners. The sequence of allocations is the following:

- B4 is allocated 15 (10 + 5) units.
- B3 is allocated 20 units.
- B2 is allocated 20 units.
- B6 is allocated 15 units.
- B5 is allocated 20 units.
- B1 is allocated 10 units

Since demand exceeds supply, it is obvious that all the resources offered by the providers will be allocated to the auction winners. What remains to be decided is what units are allocated to which bidder, i.e. the mapping of providers' units to user allocations. As also stated previously, the objective is clearly to mitigate the switching costs of the auction winners and allow them to make efficient use of the adjacent spectrum frequencies' guard band. Therefore, the winner determination phase must take into account this constraint by ensuring that the minimum number of providers allocates units to each winner. Therefore, in the aforementioned example, the allocations will be as follows:

- The 25 units of P1 will be allocated to B1 (10 units) and B4 (15 units).
- The 35 units of P2 will be allocated to B5 (20 units) and B6 (15 units).
- The remaining 40 units of P3 are to be allocated to B2 and B3 (20 units each).

This way, the number of providers per customer is minimized (in this example it is 1, which is the ideal case).

The computation of the attained revenue is depicted below.

Table 6.4. The attained revenue of the auction

The Auction Revenue	
Total Revenue:	$(10+20)*9 + (20+15+20)*8 + 10*7 + 5*6 = €810$
P1 Revenue:	$(25 * 810 / 100) = €202.5$
P2 Revenue:	$(35 * 810 / 100) = €283.5$
P3 Revenue:	$(40 * 810 / 100) = €324$

The example presented above corresponds to the general case where demand exceeds supply. Next we consider an example where demand is low and thus is exceeded by supply. In particular, we consider the previous example with the twist that only bidders B1, B2 and B6 are present and that they place the same bids as before. That is the bids are now as presented in the table to follows, asking for a total of 65 units.

Next, the auction software allocates the specific units to the auction winners, starting from the highest bids. The sequence of allocations decided by the marketplace is the following:

- B3 is allocated 20 units.
- B6 is allocated 15 units.
- B1 is allocated 10 units.
- B1 is allocated 5 units.
- B3 is allocated 10 units.

Bidder	Quantity (units)	Per-unit Price (€)
B1	10	7
B1	5	5
B6	15	8
B3	20	9
B3	10	3

Note that under this scenario, the total demand is 60 units, which is 60% of the total supply (namely, 100 units). Thus, ideally, for each of the three providers, 60% of their units should be granted. Therefore, 0.6 * 25 = 15 units of P1, 0.6 * 35 = 21 units of P2 and 0.6 * 40 = 24 units of P3 will be allocated to the auction winners. In order to minimize the winners' switching costs a possible allocation is the following:

- The 15 units of P1 are allocated to B1. Therefore, B1 is fully served by P1.
- 15 out of 21 units of P2 are allocated to B6. Therefore, B6 is fully served by P2.

The remaining 6 units of P2 and the 24 units of P3 are allocated to B3, who will be served by two providers. Note that the latter is inevitable, due to the fact that there is no provider that can alone provide the large quantity of resources won by B6. The computation of the attained revenue is depicted below.

The Auction Revenue	
Total Revenue:	20*9 + 15*8 + 10*7 + 5*5+5*3 = €410
P1 Revenue:	(15 * 410 / 60) = €102.5
P2 Revenue:	(21 * 410 / 60) = €143.5
P3 Revenue:	(24 * 410 / 60) = €164

CONCLUSION

In this chapter, we have discussed the use of auctions in electronic markets. A presentation of the adoption of auctions in various kinds of marketplaces and electronic systems is provided. The main features of the auctions adopted for electronic markets have been briefly mentioned and their differences with respective to the theoretical definition of those mechanisms have been highlighted and intuitively explained. Subsequently, we have focused on the use of auctions in electronic markets that are used by telecom providers for the lease of telecommunication assets.

Finally, an indicative auction design that could be adopted for a telecom spectrum market and a comprehensive execution example of this auction are presented. In particular, we have opted for a multi-unit sealed-bid auction with a pay-your-bid payment rule. This is a design intentionally kept simple, which however fails to express the complementarities that exist for allocation of spectrum over time; this will be revisited in the two penultimate chapters of this book.

Overall, the adoption of auctions for electronic auctions is prominent and is expected to be intensified in the near future.

REFERENCES

[1]   Ebay, URL: http://www.ebay.com/.
[2]   Ashenfelter, O., How Auctions Work for Wine and Art, *The Journal of Economic Prespectives*, 3:3, 23-36, 1989.
[3]   Van Heck, E.; Ribbers, P. Experiences with Electronic Auctions in the Dutch Flower Industry, *Global Electronic Commerce: Theory and Case Studies*, 355—366, The MIT Press, Cambridge, MA, 1999.
[4]   Arbinet, URL: www.arbinet.com

[5]   eSwitch, URL: http://eswitch.com.au/

[6]   Invisible hand report, URL: http://web.invisiblehand.net/ihn-bmr/.

[7]   The Yahoo Telecommunications Directory, Bandwidth Auctions
       and Exchanges, URL: http://dir.yahoo.com/Business_and_Economy
       /Business_to_Business/Communications_and_Networking/Telecommun
       ications/Bandwidth_Auctions_and_Exchanges/

[8]   Internet Draft. Network based IP VPN Architecture Using Virtual
       Routers, URL: http://www.ietf.org/internet-drafts/draft-ietf-l3vpn-vpn-
       vr-03.txt.

[9]   SpecEx, URL: www.specex.com

[10]   ACMA, URL: www.acma.gov.au

[11]   Australian Communications and Media Authority, Spectrum Trading:
       Consultation on Trading and third party authorizations of spectrum and
       apparatus licenses, November 2008.

[12]   Software Defined Radio Forum, Business Models for Wireless PCS.
       Document No. SDRF-03-P-0001-V1.0.0 (formerly SDRF-03-A-
       0001-V0.00) URL: http://www.sdrforum.org/pages/documentLibrary
       /documents/SDRF-03-P-0001-V1_0_0_Business_Case.pdf

[13]   URL: http://www.ofcom.org.uk/radiocomms/.

[14]   Ausubel, L.; Cramton, P. Demand Reduction and Inefficiency in multi-
       unit auctions. Working paper, No 96-07, Univ. of Maryland, 1996,
       URL: http://www.ausubel.com/larry/auction-papers.htm

Chapter 7

GRID, ECONOMICS AND AUCTION THEORY

ABSTRACT

Over the past years there has been an increasing interest in economic-aware Grid systems. In particular, new commercial Grid markets have evolved, where Grid resources and services are offered to the public, as opposed to the academia-oriented legacy processor sharing systems of the recent past. No surprise, there have been many research proposals regarding the design of economic mechanisms for the allocation of Grid resources to users that demand to lease them over a certain time interval with auctions being the primary candidate. This chapter presents a classification of the plethora of economic mechanisms that have been proposed in the literature for computational Grids. It also presents both the merits and the limitations of these mechanisms, as well as their fitness in different contexts, thus performing an assessment of the proposed in the literature game-theoretic and auction mechanisms. Finally, it presents a set of additional issues that are of prominent importance for economic-aware Grid systems. Hopefully, this discussion clarifies what types of mechanisms would be both meaningful and practically applicable for the various types of computational Grids, thus providing insight on what game-theoretic and auction mechanisms would be likely to evolve in real-world Grid systems.

INTRODUCTION

Evolving from the electricity grids and the time-sharing computational systems of the recent past, economic-aware Grid systems have been the center of attention for both the academia and the industry over the last years. The term *grid computing* has been used to describe the use of a multitude of computing elements, possibly from different geographic locations and of different ownership, that collectively execute a user application or attempt to solve a scientific problem. It is the evolution of the large academic processor systems of the past. The term *cloud computing* is also common in the literature and refers to commercial systems providing computational power over the Internet, i.e. the "Internet cloud".

There has been an increasing interest in Grid services, market architectures and commercial Grid systems [1]. In order to facilitate the trading of Grid resources, thus allowing a wide-scale sharing of computational resources, a variety of virtualization platforms and related business models for Grid computing have been developed.

Furthermore, economic-aware Grid systems have become increasingly popular both in the industry [2], [3], [4] and the academia [5], [6], [7], [8], [9], [10], [11], [12], [13]. Industry focuses on the economic mechanisms in an effort to assess the gains from investing in Grid technology, either as a grid (added-value) services provider, or by mitigating computational infrastructure expenses. Research efforts concentrate on designing Grid market mechanisms. These mechanisms should ensure the viability, the robustness and the efficiency of the Grid.

No surprise, a plethora of Grid markets and economic-aware Grid systems has been proposed. The typical Grid architecture of these works involves a number of grid service providers and customers that interact either directly or via agents through an either centralized or distributed marketplace.

In this context, there have been numerous research proposals on Grid economic-aware systems based on fixed prices, bartering, negotiations and/or auction models for leasing "Grid contracts". A detailed overview, presentation and classification of the economic-aware computational grids can be found in [14].

However, despite the plethora of economic mechanisms that have been proposed for the Grid market, very few efforts have been made to fully specify the design of a market that is tailored to the Grid products and services. Indeed, most research works attempt to straightforwardly apply well-known economic mechanisms in the Grid context, without taking into account the inherent features of the Grid and their impact on users' strategies. For instance, most proposals neglect taking into account the fact that both the *resource type* and the *time dimension* are of significant importance for the Grid market resources and actors.

This chapter performs a classification of the economic mechanisms that have been proposed for economic-aware computational Grids and illustrates both the merits and the limitations of these approaches. Hence, this chapter performs an assessment of the proposed mechanisms, which clarifies what types of mechanisms would be both meaningful and practically applicable for the various types of computational Grids. Finally, it presents a set of additional issues that are of prominent importance for economic-aware Grid systems. We argue that the presentation of these issues can provide useful insight on what game-theoretic and auction mechanisms would be likely to evolve in real-world Grid systems. We argue that the presentation of these issues can provide useful insight on what game-theoretic and auction mechanisms would be likely to evolve in real-world Grid systems.

Note that understanding both the limitations and the potential applicability of the economic mechanisms proposed for the Grid is extremely important. In fact, there have been quite many cases in the recent past where bad mechanism design had dramatic effects on the performance of various markets in the context of electricity and telecommunications. The most prominent cases of such cases is the bad market design of the California power market, which led to the market's collapse [15], and the "fiasco'" [16] of the Turkish UMTS auction where bad auction design led to a monopoly of the Turkish 3G market and a subsequent cancellation of the auction by the regulator. In order to mitigate the threat of bad mechanism design, it is necessary to perform a per-case in-depth study of the various economic models and identify their respective merits and drawbacks. This analysis can then motivate the Grid market design decisions to be taken.

The remainder of this chapter is structured as follows: First, we present the state of the art in economic mechanisms proposed for economic-aware computational Grids. Subsequently, we discuss the limitations, the pros and the cons of these mechanisms for the Grid, present some additional important issues that are of importance for Grid mechanism design and highlight these issues impact on the Grid (auction) mechanism design decisions. Finally, we provide some concluding remarks.

GRID ECONOMIC MODELS AND MECHANISMS

This section contains a broad classification of the economic models and mechanisms proposed for economic-aware computational Grids. For brevity reasons, we refrain from providing a detailed presentation of all the economic-aware Grid systems. Instead, in this chapter we focus on the mechanisms proposed in these works, providing indicative references thereof, and discuss their suitability to economic-aware computational Grids. Most research works on Grid mechanism design are oriented towards defining a very simple elementary resource, which is the basic unit of trade of the computational economy. The most widely used definition is that of CPU cycles. Another definition is that of a virtual machine (VM), i.e. a CPU of a certain processing power and configuration. Note that there is a significant economic advantage of the second approach, i.e. that of definition of certain VM types, which can be leased: In particular, this definition indicates that the core of the market is *computational service*, rather than raw computational elements.

This distinction is important, since it reflects a more service-oriented economic-aware approach. Indeed, computational services are of *well-defined economic value* to the Grid market participants, as opposed to the vague value of quantities of raw computation elements. There has been extensive work on what kind of pricing mechanisms should be used. The most prominent proposal so far is that of auctions. In particular, there are research works that have more or less proposed that any kind of auction is suitable for the Grid (English, Dutch, Double, combinatorial and Vickrey auctions) and present a comparative "assessment" of these auction formats. Surprisingly, the vast majority of these works neglect to assess those mechanisms in economic terms. That is, no study is performed for the implications of the market design to users' participation and strategies in the market, the user constraints and time limitations in supply and demand for resources are nowhere taken into account in the model, the demand generated for the simulations is implicitly assumed to be price-insensitive. Overall, the discussion is limited to comparison of computational and message overhead as well as of the attained "prices" and "revenue". A typical example of such an approach is that of [17].

Excluding bartering and schemes that do not involve the exchange of money among the Grid economy participants, the remaining proposed economic models for the Grid market could be classified as follows:

Commodity Market

Under this approach, it is assumed that there is a single homogeneous good that is to be sold through the market. Hence, no differentiation among resources is feasible.

Commodity market relies on the notion of a market price for the good sold. In the context of Grid, this price is publicly announced to the actors of the Grid market; this price can be:

a) *Fixed*: This is the simplest pricing policy where the price for a certain service, e.g. the leasing of a virtual machine (VM) of a certain type, is fixed. Fixed prices are simple and popular among the existing oligopolistic commercial Grid providers [2], [3].

b) *Variable*: Under this scheme the price fluctuates to reflect the demand and supply fluctuations over time [5].

Proportional Fairness

This scheme prescribes that a *share auction* takes place for the Grid resources. In particular, consumers place bids for the Grid resource and the winner determination rule prescribes that each user is allocated the fair share of the total resources available. The economic motivation behind this scheme is that for logarithmic user utility functions, this scheme is both Pareto-optimal and socially efficient.

Tycoon [18] is the prominent computational Grid system employing this scheme, while Libra [12] is a similar academic effort.

Auctions and Reverse Auctions

This is the dominant mechanism proposed in the literature (e.g. see [7], [10], [11], [17]). Auctions are market mechanisms that rely on the submission of bids from the consumers for the good auctioned by the provider. It implicitly assumes synchronization of all the consumers and the bidding regards only the price.Auctions can be either provider-initiated where the highest bidders are awarded the auctioned items or consumer-initiated. The latter family of auctions is called *reverse auctions* and the winner is the provider who demands the least money for servicing the customer. For consumer-initiated auctions, typically a contract specifying the job to be executed, the quantity of resources needed as well as the job's respective time deadline is procured.

Negotiations

This can be seen as a special case of auctions where two parties negotiate over a Grid "contract". This negotiation can be in general multi-parametric, concerning a set of attributes of the contract and not just the price. As opposed to the auction bidding process, the negotiation process is in general asynchronous and relies on the exchange of offers and counter-offers between the two parties, possibly by means of agents in an effort to speed up the negotiation process [19].

Negotiations have been proposed as a means of trade and interaction of large Grid actors (e.g. a commercial Grid provider and a large bank whose needs for computation are very high) [7], [20].

Spot Markets

Spot markets employ a bid-and-ask mechanism, i.e. a continuous double auction. This mechanism prescribes that consumers denote their demand by submitting multiple bids, while providers denote their supply by submitting multiple asks.

The rationale of the bid-and-ask mechanism prescribes that the highest bid is matched with the lowest ask(s) that are active in the market; this procedure is repeated until all possible matches are made. Spot markets have been widely and successfully used in electricity, crude oil trading and stock markets (e.g. the NYSE).

Constrained Optimization

This category comprises of mechanisms and systems where a certain optimization problem is solved in order to maximize a certain performance metric, such as maximization of number of jobs executed, minimization of average delay (see [9], [14], [21], and references therein).

FITNESS/IMPACT OF THE ECONOMIC MECHANISMS TO GRID

Having completed the presentation of the proposed in the literature economic mechanisms for the Grid, we proceed to discuss the limitations, the merits, the pros and cons of adopting those schemes for computational Grids.

Commodity market

Commodity markets are widely used in economics. The benefits of this approach stem from a fundamental assumption, that of *perfect competition*. That is, it is assumed that all market actors, both consumers and *producers*, have a small fraction of the total market share. This way, they cannot affect the market price by means of a strategy, thus the market is perfectly competitive and all agents are price-takers. It is clear that this assumption does not hold in the existing oligopolistic commercial Grid environment where few large providers dominate the market [2], [3].

Therefore, the adoption of such a mechanism for commercial B2C grids would be only beneficial for the few large commercial providers who control the market and the prices. No surprise, this is the pricing scheme adopted from providers like Amazon [2] and Sun [3] who aim to control the market.

However, commodity markets could perform well in B2B intra-grids or academic grids where there are no large asymmetries between the partners in terms of both the type and quantity of resources owned, which are shared by means of the Grid infrastructure.

Moreover, this approach suffers from the same drawbacks of the auctions approach, except that of market instability. However, the centralized approach of this scheme may not be reasonable for large Grids. Also, if the price is fixed, this scheme is inefficient due to variation of demand and supply over time, which is not reflected to the market price. Moreover, the fact that one homogeneous good is to be sold limits the potential for product differentiation and prohibits the expression of time constraints in demand and supply, which are of prominent importance for the Grid.

Last but not least, assuming perfect information for the Grid, the price-setting mechanism of the commodity markets is known to lead to price wars and lemon markets [22]; both these phenomena are highly undesirable since they result in cut-throat competition which overall reduces the choices of the customers and the efficiency of the market.

Proportional Fairness

Proportional fairness schemes rely on a central coordination point, which is aware of the total quantity of available identical resources and also collects the bids of consumers for resources. It subsequently splits the resources available proportionally to users' bids. The main drawback of this approach is that it involves uncertainty. Consumers have no way to predict what quantity of resources they will be allocated and whether these will suffice to complete their respective tasks in time. Thus, they are vulnerable to the *exposure problem*. This means that it is probable that customers may end up being awarded only subsets of the resources needed in order to complete their tasks on time and being charged for them more highly than the respective utility obtained for the fraction of tasks being executed by means of utilizing the awarded resources.

Also under high load, the fair share of every user is expected to be a small fraction of the total resources, thus increasing the probability that anyone will manage to complete the execution of his tasks in time. Therefore, this scheme involves *uncertainty* for consumers and cannot cope with time deadlines. Therefore, it is not suitable for computational Grids where the economic value stems from the fact that certain jobs are executed within certain time deadlines. In fact, the proportional fairness scheme can be seen as a remainder of the processor sharing systems of the recent past, and are not well suited for economic-aware commercial Grids.

Auctions and Reverse Auctions

Auctions are relevant because they are known to perform well in terms of revenue and social welfare attained in cases of incomplete information. In the Grid context this is the case regarding a series of factors, such as the actual demand and supply and their respective price elasticity, the consumers' value for reserving various quantities of resources, the resource providers' actual costs, the urgency of the expressed demand and the flexibility of supply with respect to time constraints.

However, auctions' performance may be poor in terms of revenue in cases of low demand, where even zero-price equilibria are likely to appear. Also, the existence of a central auction for the entire Grid's resources has significant overhead and would imply that all (identical) resources are auctioned for the same time interval of lease; thus, it fails to express the different time constraints of the providers and consumers.

On the other hand, if a distributed approach is adopted, i.e. a variety of local auctions are initiated by the market's participants in a distributed fashion for the resources owned/desired, this may result in unfairness, undesirable large price fluctuations and instability of the market. It might be very difficult for consumers to choose on which auction to bid and users bidding in many auctions face the exposure problem. Furthermore, due to different participation in the various auctions, price dispersion is expected to be significant. Last but not least, if few large participants dominate the market, it is possible for them to manipulate the resulting market allocations and prices [15].

Furthermore, it is worth noting that some of the auction mechanisms proposed for the Grid, such as Vickrey auctions, rely on assuming continuous twice-differentiable utility/cost functions.This is proven not to be the case in electricity markets where discontinuous step functions are the norm; this could be the case also for Grid providers. Therefore, applying such mechanisms entails the risk of unpredictably bad performance of the market, as was the case in the California power market. Moreover, the optimal bidding function even for single-unit auctions in cases where the number of participants is a priori unknown is extremely complex, since it is actually a weighted sum over all possible numbers of bidders of the respective optimal bidding function.

To make things worse, these bidding functions are proven not to be optimal in cases where the auction is repeated often or under multi-unit demand and supply. Finally, the performance of these mechanisms depends heavily on a plethora of parameters and there is not a "one-fit-all" solution. Thus, it is practically impossible to predict the optimal bidding function and the respective values of the expected revenue and the social welfare attained in the Grid context if auctions are adopted.

Moreover, the complexity of the Vickrey auction and that of combinatorial mechanisms are known to be in general NP-hard, thus mitigating their applicability in practice. Also, note that combinatorial auctions require that all items put up for sale are discriminatory; such an approach clearly limits the liquidity of the market and increases the mechanism's complexity.

Finally, the fact that many of these mechanisms, namely all the sealed-bid mechanisms and the Dutch and combinatorial auctions, require that the bidder reveals his maximum willingness to pay for certain quantities or combinations of resources may be undesirable for consumers who may fear that this information could be used by the Grid providers in subsequent auctions in order e.g. to set high reserve prices for the resources offered. Thus, *entry deterrence* may further mitigate competition and the respective expected revenue.

Negotiations

Bilateral or multilateral negotiation mechanisms are well suited for the context of Grid. Negotiations produce satisfactory revenue even in the case of low market demand for resources and poly-parametric negotiations capture better the market's externalities. They are easier to implement than auctions, have less administrative and logistics overhead than auctions, but are also more difficult to model and in general the negotiation process is time consuming. Also, due to their distributed nature and the imperfect market information, it is likely that they fail to maximize social welfare, due to the fact that they regard local decisions made under incomplete information, which are not system-wide optimal.

However, the negotiation process is far more time consuming and often difficult to automate. Also, it often is associated with excessive message overhead and does not scale up well with number of users and transactions performed. Concluding, this appears to be an approach that would work in B2B Grids for few participants who want to interact with low frequency in order to make some big deals. Therefore, this scheme could be of some limited use in B2B grids.

Spot Markets

As already explained, the main merit of employing a spot market, i.e. a continuous double auction where both providers and consumers of resources express their supply and demand respectively by means of asks and bids is the simplicity, popularity and provable efficiency of the bid-and-ask mechanism. A straightforward application of the spot market would prescribe that computational power is dynamically leased for short time intervals and the contract would be fulfilled according to the "as soon as possible" rationale of the bid-and-ask mechanism. Note that this is the standard practice in trading of crude oil. A slight variation exists in the context of electricity where power is traded over predefined slots of fixed duration. Finally, the spot markets used in stock markets are used for the exchange of the *ownership* of stocks, as opposed to the *leasing* of the Grid resources for some time.

It is clear that a straightforward application of all these variations in the Grid context would neglect the fact that the time dimension for the leasing of Grid resources over multiple time intervals is of prominent importance. Indeed, providers of resources such as data centers can only make resources available during the time that these are idle; the latter depends on their internal scheduling flexibility. Also, consumers need to lease a certain amount of resources up to a certain deadline in order to execute a certain task; this could be the leasing of additional computational power in times of high demand for a company's web server or the execution of a stock market time series forecast up to the opening time of the stock markets.

Therefore, it is important to enrich the bid-and-ask mechanism of the traditional spot markets with time deadlines; this way bids and asks also declare a maximum deadline up to which resources must be made available or are offered respectively. This is a promising novel approach that was adopted in the GridEcon project [23]. We argue that such an approach limits the uncertainty of the market participants since there is no exposure problem, while it facilitates the growth of the Grid since anyone can be a Grid market participant as a provider or consumer of resources or both.

Similar issues and arguments apply for the futures market as well. Finally, it is worth noting that the co-existence of the spot and future market is beneficial from an economic point of view. The futures market can be seen as the tool for performing long-term IT planning, while the spot market can be used for accommodating urgent needs or customer demand spikes of a business. Note that this is nicely complemented with the capacity planner functionality, which can further assist an SME lease computational power when needed and in an optimal fashion. This is crucial to mitigate infrastructure expenditure and assist SMEs to efficiently invest and utilize the Grid infrastructure by means of any marketplace. Needless to say, this is highly beneficial especially in times of economic crisis.

Constrained Optimization

This approach is mostly a theoretical construct, which could be of some value to the processor sharing systems of the recent past, but is of limited applicability to generic Grid systems where a multitude of competing applications coincide; these applications have typically conflicting performance goals that are to be met. Besides the centralized nature and the computational overhead of this approach, its major drawback is that the relationship between the system optimization goal and the actual desires of the users remains vague. Such approaches neglect taking into account user preferences and are not applicable to real-world computational Grids.

Additional Considerations

Some important issues that distinguish Grid from traditional distributed systems and economic models such as those used in electricity and stock markets, which also affect the Grid mechanism design problem, are presented here.

The most prominent issue is that the *time dimension* of leasing of resources is of significant importance. In general, the fact that not ownership but leasing for a certain interval of computational service is traded, greatly complicates both the design and analysis of Grid mechanisms.

Also, depending on the type of computational Grid, it is not clear whether there is a clear distinction between consumers and producers; a company may be a provider in time periods where its resources are underutilized and a consumer during times where it needs additional resources. These issues are expected to have a significant impact on the Grid market actors' strategies, but are absent in existing economic models.

Also the immediate urgency and price-insensitivity of demand of the electricity market seem to be absent in the Grid context, thus enabling more efficient schemes for multiplexing and shaping of demand and supply.

Finally, issues such as risk brokering, insurance policies to mitigate uncertainty, capacity planning, security, reputation and trust mechanisms are complementary factors of high impact to the Grid mechanism design problem. These mechanisms and services complement the basic economic model used for the trading of computational resources in order to mitigate the markets participants' risk and uncertainty.

CONCLUSION

We have presented a classification of the plethora of economic mechanisms that have been proposed in the literature for computational Grids. We have discussed both the merits and the limitations of these mechanisms, thus performing a comparative assessment of them in terms of their fitness to the Grid. We have elaborated that a limited set of those mechanisms are both of value and practically applicable to real Grid systems. Furthermore, we have briefly presented some additional issues that are of high importance for economic-aware Grid systems and are worth to be further investigated. Concluding, this chapter clarifies what types of mechanisms would be both meaningful and practically applicable for economic-aware computational Grids and highlights some interesting topics for future research in the open problem of Grid mechanism design.

REFERENCES

[1]   Armstrong, M.; Baxter, R. A Complete History of the Grid. URL: http://www.nesc.ac.uk/action/esi/download.cfm?index=353.

[2]   Amazon Elastic Compute Cloud (Amazon EC2), URL: http://aws. amazon.com/ec2/.

[3]   SunGrid, URL: http://www.sun.com/software/gridware/

[4]   HP grid, URL: http://h20338.www2.hp.com/enterprise/cache/250417-0-0-0-121.html

[5]   Nabrzyski, J.; Schopf, M.; Weglarz, J. Grid Resource Management: State of the Art and Future Trends, Kluwer Academic Publishers, 2004.

[6]   EGEE, URL: http://egee1.eu-egee.org/.

[7]   SORMA, URL: http://sorma-project.org/.

[8]   Grid5000, URL: https://www.grid5000.fr/mediawiki/index.php/Grid 5000:Home

[9]   The Grid Economy Project, URL: http://www.gridbus.org/ecogrid/

[10]   GRIA: Service Oriented Collaborations for Industry and Commerce, URL: http://www.gria.org/

[11]   AuYoung, A.; Chun, B.; Snoeren, A.; Vahdat, A. Resource allocation in federated distributed computing infrastructures. *Proc. of the 1st Workshop on Operating System and Architectural Support for the On demand IT InfraStructure*, Oct, 2004.

[12] Sherwani, J.; Ali, N.; Lotia, N.; Hayat, Z.; Buyya, R. Libra: a computational economy-based job scheduling system for clusters. *Software: Practice and Experience*, vol. 34, pp. 573-590, 2004.

[13]] Buyya, R., Abramson, D.; Giddy, J.; Stockinger, H. Economic models for resource management and scheduling in Grid computing. *Concurrency and Computation: Practice and Experience*, vol. 14, pp. 1507-1542, 2002.

[14] The GridEcon project consortium, GridEcon Deliverable D2.1: Economic Modelling Requirement Report, 2008.

[15] Hogan, W. The California Meltdown. *Harvard Magazine*, Sept. 2001, URL: http://ksghome.harvard.edu/~whogan/harvard_hogan0901.pdf

[16] Klemperer, P. What Really Matters in Auction Design. *Journal of Economic Perspectives*, vol. 16:1, pp. 169-189, Dec 2002.

[17] Broberg, J. Venugopal, S.; Buyya, R. Market-oriented Grids and Utility Computing: The State-of-the-art and Future Directions. *Journal of Grid Computing*, vol. 6:3, pp. 255-276, Dec. 2007.

[18] Broberg, J. Venugopal, S.; Buyya, R. Tycoon: An implementation of a distributed, market-based resource allocation system. *Multiagent and Grid Systems*, vol. 1:3, pp. 169-182, Aug. 2005

[19] Bichler, M.; Kersten, G.; Strecker, S. Towards a Structured Design of Electronic Negotiations. *Group Decision and Negotiation*, vol. 12:4, pp. 311-335, 2003.

[20] BEinGRID: Business experiments in Grids, URL: http://www. beingrid.eu/

[21] Krauter, K.; Buyya, R.; Maheswaran, M. A Taxonomy and Survey of Grid Resource Management Systems for Distributed Computing. *Software Practice and Experience*, vol. 32, pp. 135-164, 2002.

[22] IBM Information Economies Project: Research Papers, URL: http://www.research.ibm.com/infoecon/researchpapers.html

[23] [7.23] The GridEcon Project, URL: http://www.gridecon.eu

Chapter 8

AUCTION MECHANISMS FOR ALLOCATING THE BANDWIDTH OF A NETWORK TO ITS USERS

ABSTRACT

The rapid growth of Internet has resulted in increased need for bandwidth. At the same time, the introduction of innovative technologies, such as optical fibres, wireless and satellite links, has increased the supply of bandwidth, which is now offered at lower prices. However, at parts of the network such as the interconnection points and the transatlantic links bandwidth remains a scarce and costly resource. This chapter presents the main issues and mechanisms of auction-based resource allocation in telecom networks. It formulates the problem of network bandwidth allocation, studies its aspects, and finally presents and assesses the mechanisms proposed in the literature with respect to both their theoretical properties/merits and their potential applicability to real networks or bandwidth markets.

INTRODUCTION

The rapid growth of Internet has resulted in increased need for bandwidth. At the same time, the introduction of innovative technologies, such as optical fibres, wireless and satellite links, has increased the supply of bandwidth, which is now offered at lower prices. Moreover, due to increased competition among providers, customized short-term bandwidth contracts are now preferred by users to static, long-term contracts of the past. Furthermore, at parts of the network such as the interconnection points and the transatlantic links, bandwidth remains a scarce and costly resource. These facts have created an overwhelming interest in dynamic bandwidth brokering applications.

Auctions offer the advantages of: i) simplicity in determining market-based prices, and ii) efficiency, since, if the auction is properly designed, goods are acquired by those that value them most. Furthermore, auctions may lead to higher revenues for the providers compared to traditional methods of selling goods. As already explained earlier in this book, there are multiple ways to classify auctions and besides the well-known simple auction formats, (i.e. English, Dutch, First-price sealed, and Vickrey), there are numerous variations thereof. Though such auction mechanisms can be adopted for allocating the bandwidth of just a single link, they cannot be applied to the case of networks.

Thus, "standard" auction theory is lacking an auction-based self-regulating, efficient and fair mechanism for bandwidth allocation in a network. Such a mechanism could be very useful in practice. In particular, it could be adopted by the bandwidth markets so as to enable their customers to dynamically build end-to-end paths, or multicast trees, or complex Virtual Private Networks (VPNs) of arbitrary topology by means of a network-scale coordination and allocation mechanism. Such an auction mechanism could also be used as an internal bandwidth allocation mechanism for networks interconnecting academic and research institutes, i.e. the NRENs, where attaining revenue is not the primary goal.

This book chapter is dedicated to presenting some attempts to address this issue by means of devising auction-based resource allocation mechanisms. It is worth emphasizing that we refrain from presenting alternative - to auctions - ways of allocating bandwidth, since this book restricts attention to how auctions can be applied in telecoms-related problems.

AUCTIONING THE BANDWIDTH OF A NETWORK

This section formulates the problem of bandwidth allocation of a network. It highlights the main problem aspects and constraints that should be met by any solution proposed that attempts to address this problem.

Let us assume that there are N links whose bandwidth is being auctioned simultaneously and I users bidding for bandwidth over paths of the network.

This bandwidth will be utilized by all users for the same period; this last assumption will be relaxed later. When bandwidth is auctioned, users must be incentivized to reveal their true needs in terms of quantity bandwidth and willingness to pay. Thus, an auction mechanism sets prices that reflect the state of the market. Such a mechanism is known to be particularly useful in markets of heterogeneous users with highly scattered and unknown valuations, which is the case with users placing their bids over Internet.

A meaningful set of objectives regarding any suitable auction-based network bandwidth allocation mechanism follows:

- Each user should be able buy the *same* quantity of bandwidth capacity in all the links he is bidding for. This goal is very important, since buying a path with different bandwidth at its constituent links is useless for the buyer and inefficient. Note that similar constraints apply if different quantities of bandwidth are to be purchased on top of a network in order to build a Virtual Private Network (VPN) of arbitrary topology or a multicast tree; this is essentially a different formulation of the same problem that should be dealt with by an auction mechanism. This objective constitutes the main difference between the problem of this chapter and the "traditional" multi-unit auction. Indeed, assume that in each link bandwidth is sold in units. Then, the objective of path formation imposes constraints regarding which combinations of goods (i.e. bandwidth units) are acceptable by each user in the final allocation, thus rendering traditional multi-unit auction mechanisms inapplicable.

- The overall allocation of bandwidth attained by auction should be *efficient*, i.e. maximize social welfare. That is, bandwidth should be acquired by those that need it the most. In fact, this is the primary goal when the auction is to be applied as an internal allocation mechanism; e.g., a large institution can use it to allocate bandwidth over its VPN to the institution's divisions.

- Each user should be charged *fairly* with respect to the quantity of bandwidth he consumes.

- In the case of a commercial network provider, the auction should result in *high revenues*. While this objective is essentially of no interest when the mechanism is only employed for the purpose of internal allocation (see example above), it is obviously very important if the provider is an entity that is independent of the users. However, a provider should never ignore the issue of efficiency; for otherwise, its users may migrate to another provider, in case they are not satisfied with the allocation attained. Henceforth, the objective of high provider's revenues shall also be consided, although efficiency is the primary goal.

- The mechanism should be *scalable* with respect to both the size of the network and the number of users. This is of great importance for the Internet where there are approximately 33,000 different networks (Autonomous Systems) and myriads of users.S
- The mechanism should be *reliable*, and *not susceptible to collusion* or dishonest dealing.
- From a practical point of view, the mechanism should be simple, intuitive, and easy to use; it should both convergence quickly to the final allocation and require small amounts of computation. This way, it is possible to apply it in practice.

Finally, we state certain technical assumptions. We assume that each user is associated with a utility function $U_i(\cdot)$ that expresses his valuation (and hence his willingness-to-pay) for quantities of bandwidth over a particular path. (Note that the terms utility and valuation will henceforth be used interchangeably.) For simplicity reasons, it is assumed that each user is interested in a single path and that the capacity of each link is infinitely divisible and can also be sold in integral units.

POSSIBLE APPROACHES FOR THE AUCTION MECHANISM

We now proceed to discuss the pros and cons of various auction mechanisms that could be used to address the problem studied in this chapter.

Combinatorial versus Simultaneous Auctions

The first major decision to be made concerns whether or not to allow users to place combinatorial bids for all the links for which they are interested in reserving bandwidth. The major advantage of a combinatorial auction is the efficient sharing of the network resources. However, there are certain problems with such an auction, due to the overlaps of users' combinations – such as the threshold and free rider problem (see Chapter 3). Its major disadvantage however is by far its high computational complexity. Winner determination is in general an NP–complete problem.

On the other hand, using simultaneous independent auctions (one per link) eliminates the above problems, but the problems of simultaneous termination of the various auctions and inefficiency in allocations due to the overlapping paths of rival users may appear. However, these issues can be mitigated successfully as explained later in this chapter. Last but not least, the use of simultaneous auctions in the FCC auction and the success of this procedure are also in favor of the latter approach.

Open versus Sealed Auctions

Another important decision regards whether the auction should be open or sealed. In the former case, bidders have access to all or some part of the information concerning the bids of others, while in the latter case each bidder places his bid on the basis of his own valuation only.

Sealed bids do not reveal much information about the market status, and thus no estimate of competition can be made by users. Thus, it is hard for users to develop an efficient strategy. Since combinatorial bids are not allowed (see previous subsection), users must place a sealed bid for each link of the path. Since there are many ways to split the total value for the path among the various links, he must decide on this arbitrarily. This makes it highly possible that he loses at a link's auction and cannot do anything about it. Similarly, bidders can waste money fearing that if they place a lower bid they may not win. Thus, a sealed auction may result in loss of money for certain bidders and/or under-utilization of bandwidth even in times of high demand. Finally, such auctions suffer from the problems of phantom bidding and dishonest dealing among the seller and certain users he wishes to favor.

An open auction does not involve these problems. Much more information is revealed and competition is promoted. Information revelation allows users to estimate the demand by others at the various links and follow a strategy. This way, reasonable prices, at the various links reflecting the actual demand are reached. Moreover, an open mechanism is more transparent and reliable.

Ascending versus Descending Auctions

The third important decision pertains to whether the link auctions should be of ascending or descending price. In an ascending auction, price is initially low and incremented until demand matches supply. On the contrary, in a descending auction, price is initially high and is gradually decreased.

In multi-unit ascending auctions, either all goods are allocated to the users when total demand matches supply, or goods are gradually "clinched" by users whenever it is definite that such a clinching is part of the final allocation. Below, we argue that the former approach is not appropriate for auctioning bandwidth in a network; this also applies for the latter, but we refrain from discussing this for brevity and simplicity of presentation reasons.

The main problem when employing an ascending auction for bandwidth in multiple links is as follows: Due to the difference in the demand per link, it is impossible to synchronize the auctions of the various links so that all of them terminate at the same time. This is rigorously proved below for a network consisting of two links with the same capacity C. For simplicity, we assume that there are three users participating in the auctions: user 1, who is interested in purchasing bandwidth in the first link; user 2, who is interested in the second link; and, user 3, who is a path user, i.e. he is interested in purchasing bandwidth in the path. Each of the users has a utility function U_i that describes his valuation for various quantities of bandwidth. The auction outcome consists of the quantities of bandwidth x_1, x_2 and x_3 purchased by the three users, and by the corresponding amounts to be paid. This outcome is efficient, if the allocation of bandwidth maximizes social welfare, subject to capacity constraints. That is, if

$$\text{Max } U_1(x_1) + U_2(x_2) + U_3(x_3)$$

$$\text{subject to } \begin{cases} x_1 + x_3 \leq C \\ x_2 + x_3 \leq C \end{cases}$$

This problem may be solved by means of Lagrange multipliers, which correspond to the per unit prices of bandwidth p_1^*, p_2^* in each link. At the efficient outcome, each user's net benefit is maximized. That is, there should hold:

$$
\begin{cases}
U_1{}'(x_1^*) = p_1^* \\
U_2{}'(x_2^*) = p_2^* \\
U_3{}'(x_3^*) = p_1^* + p_2^*
\end{cases}
\quad \text{and} \quad
\begin{cases}
p_1^*(C - x_1^* - x_3^*) = 0 \\
p_2^*(C - x_2^* - x_3^*) = 0
\end{cases}
$$

The above set of equation defines the unknown pair of prices, that when offered simultaneously at the two links lead each player to individually select such a quantity of bandwidth that the overall social welfare is maximized. Assume now that we are trying to "discover" these prices, by means of two simultaneous ascending auctions, one per link, such as the ascending clock auction. That is, the unit price in each link increases with time t, and users decrease their demand accordingly. For simplicity, we assume that users are truthful and do not apply demand reduction.

In order for such an approach to be successful, it must be ensured that the optimal pair of prices can always be offered *simultaneously* in the two links, for any set of demand functions of the three users. That is, it should always be feasible to discover dynamically a monotonic price path that terminates at the optimal point p_1^*, p_2^*. Unfortunately, this is impossible, even if the price path adapts to the demand expressed so far. In particular, in order to achieve this, the following set of inequalities hold:

$$
\begin{cases}
x_1(t) \geq x_1^* \\
x_2(t) \geq x_2^* \\
x_3(t) \geq x_3^*
\end{cases}.
$$

The objective for the provider is to attain all equalities at the same time. Since we do *not* have combinatorial bids, the bids of user 3 at the two links are placed separately, and cannot be correlated by the provider. Therefore, the only measures for the provider to assess proximity of the price path to the optimal point are $x_1(t) + x_3(t) - C$ and $x_2(t) + x_3(t) - C$, respectively. These should be positive at any time t and both reach 0 at termination. However, even if the price path adapts to these measures it cannot be guaranteed that it crosses the optimal point. For example, it may occur that $x_1(t) + x_3(t) - C > 0$ and $x_2(t) + x_3(t) - C > 0$, while $x_1(t) < x_1^*$ (due to $p_1(t) > p_1^*$), $x_3(t) > x_3^*$ (due to $p_1(t) + p_2(t) < p_1^* + p_2^*$), and $x_2(t) > x_2^*$

(due to $p_2(t) < p_2^*$). There is no way for the provider to detect such a situation, which cannot be corrected without sacrificing optimality with respect to the social welfare. This is due to the fact that the provider cannot control the three independent variables $x_1(t)$, $x_2(t)$, and $x_3(t)$ based on $x_1(t) + x_3(t) - C$ and $x_2(t) + x_3(t) - C$.

Therefore, the successful synchronization of the auctions at the optimal point is impossible. What the provider can only do in this case is once e.g. $x_1(t) + x_3(t) - C = 0$, to increase p_2 so that $x_2(t) + x_3(t) - C$ also drops to 0, while p_1 is constant. However, this will cause a decrease in $x_3(t)$ thus leaving unallocated bandwidth in link 1 or forcing path user 3 to purchase different quantities of bandwidth in the two links. This is obviously undesirable, since it causes significant waste of resources for the network and money for the users. In fact, this waste may be worse if the network is large.

We now discuss the option of descending auctions, where at every link an initial high price is set and then decreased over time. In a multi–unit Dutch auction, users' bids are immediately mapped to allocations; if a user places a bid at the sum of prices over the constituent links at some point, the quantity of resources he asks are immediately reserved and allocated to him. This way the problem of allocating the same quantity of bandwidth throughout the path for each (path) user is immediately solved by the users themselves. As for efficiency w.r.t. social welfare, it is still an issue that should be resolved by the provider.

AUCTION MECHANISMS

In this section we present the various auction mechanisms proposed in the literature for the allocation of a *network*'s bandwidth to its users. Note that we refrain to present single-link auction mechanisms, since they are clearly inadequate to address this problem.

Progressive Second Price (PSP) Auction

Auctioning bandwidth over a network has already been examined by Lazar and Semret in [1], where they present the Progressive Second Price (PSP) auction. This auction mechanism is firstly presented for the case of a single link, for which a somewhat complicated allocation rule is applied repeatedly until convergence of bids is attained: In particular, at every round users submit their bids (i.e. pairs of quantity and price) and get as feedback the bandwidth allocations they would have got if this were the final round. The current allocation is the number of units for which the user's bid has displaced rival bids, while the current charge equals the willingness to pay of the rival users for those units currently "allocated".

Bidders gradually "improve" their bids (raising the price and reducing the quantity) until demand matches supply while no bids are raised; the auction ends at this point. The idea is that each user pays so as to exactly cover the social opportunity cost, which is given by the declared willingness to pay (bids) of the users who are excluded due to his presence. PSP is only applicable for users with concave utility functions.

This mechanism is then extended to the case of a network, for which it is implicitly assumed that a bidder splits equally his bid among the links that constitute the corresponding path. This is far from being intuitive, especially since in networks it is commonly known that there are links (bottleneck links) that exhibit high demand, while competition in other links of the network is far more limited.

However, there are multiple problems with this mechanism, as the related literature indicates. PSP requires a long, computationally expensive iterative process until convergence is achieved, that results in significant message overhead for the network.

Moreover, the PSP auction, even for one link, has multiple equilibria, which can lead to an unfair result, while its "truthful equilibrium" (PSP's main merit) is unlikely to appear in practice since the fist user bidding has an obvious incentive to deviate from it, rendering its appearance in practice impossible. In particular, it is proved in [2], that the first bidder has no incentive to give his true valuation of the bandwidth; it is more beneficial for him to declare a very high willingness to pay for the link's capacity. By doing so, other bidders are prevented from bidding and the first bidder is awarded the entire link for a very small price - the link's reserve price. Though a solution to this problem is proposed by Maillé by means of enabling bidders to place truthful "sanction" losing bids, users have no incentive for submitting such truthful bids. Also in [3] it is proven that there are other equilibria of this mechanism that are more beneficial to the bidders.

Moreover, PSP requires that all the bidders bid with the same order until the auction ends and cannot cope with dynamic arrivals/departures of users, thus rendering it further impracticable. Also, the problem of enforcing the simultaneous termination of the various link auctions is not addressed by the authors that propose PSP and it remains questionable whether PSP can be indeed generalized for the network case. Finally, its high complexity results and lack of scalability result in a non-intuitive mechanism for bidders.

Multi-Bid

Motivated by the shortcomings of PSP, Tuffin and Maillé propose the multi-bid auction [4], a sealed-bid auction that is an elegant discretization of the PSP auction in sealed format *for one link*. This mechanism has also been extended for *networks of tree topology*, such as the access networks [5].

The main idea of the multi-bid auction is that a pre-specified number of bids can be submitted by the bidders in a sealed-bid auction mechanism, which is by construction essentially the PSP auction in sealed-bid format. It is proved that the same with PSP incentive compatibility properties hold under the standard PSP assumptions plus the assumption that bidders have no way to estimate the market price of the auction. It is proved that users are better off by bidding truthfully and they essentially submit discretized points of their demand function.

In particular, the bidders submit M_i pairs of quantity and respective willingness to pay per unit. It is proven that it is best for users to attempt a truthful discretization of their demand function by means of submitting M_i such truthful demand points. In practice, assuming that bidders have no idea of the market price, they choose these points so as to make sure that regardless of which bid shall be winning – depending on the quantity of units that the user will manage to get – the respective loss of surplus (the shaded surface of the figure below) is same for all bids.

Furthermore, in [5], where the problem of auctioning the bandwidth of *networks of tree topology* is addressed, the authors run an instance of the "single-link" multi-bid auction at every link of the tree, while a centralized algorithm ensures that the users will finally reserve the same quantity of bandwidth throughout their path.

The auction's computational complexity per link is a quadratic function of the number of bidders at this link. The fact that a centralized algorithm is used, combined with the fact that the multi-bid auction's complexity depends on the number of bidders, limit its scalability. Most importantly, there is no generalization of the multi-bid auction for the *general network case*.

Midas

Midas [6], [7] is motivated by the discussion of this chapter regarding the conflicting properties of the various auction mechanism decisions. In particular, MIDAS comprises of a set of simultaneous descending-price (Dutch) auctions, one per link. The name of this auction is actually an acronym which stands for **M**ulti-unit **I**ndependent **D**utch **A**uction**S**. Though the execution of the link auctions is performed with local information only, and thus in a both independent and distributed way, demand exhibited in the various links is obviously coupled due to the presence of path bidders.

In particular MIDAS works as follows:

For each link l, the link's bandwidth to be auctioned C_l as well as a high initial per unit price $p_l(0)$ are announced. Prices are gradually decreased and path bidders simultaneously bid for reserving bandwidth at the links of interest, once the link prices allow them to do so. Once a bid is accepted, this is instantly mapped to allocation, thus there is no uncertainty for the bidders whether these units will be finally allocated to them or not. This way, MIDAS solves in a smart way the problem of simultaneous termination of the auction. However, it is also important that the link prices are not reduced symmetrically (i.e. the same price should not be offered for all the links) due to the varying demand among the links.

To this end, MIDAS relies on a price reduction policy that reduces each link's price according to the demand exhibited for this link. This price reduction policy, introduced and assessed in [6] is called *Price Freezing Policy*. Its main idea is that price at each link is reduced according to a rate r, common for all links. However, when bandwidth is reserved at some link, the price for that link is "frozen" for some time, which is proportional to the units of bandwidth x_l reserved at link l. That is, the price is frozen for time $s \cdot x_l$.

Thus, when a link's l price is not frozen, it is that $p_l(t) = p_l(0) - r \cdot [t - s \cdot x_l(t)]$, where $p_l(0)$ is the initial price, $x_l(t)$ the units of bandwidth reserved at link l at time t.

Table 8.1. The MIDAS price freezing policy

Link 1	Link 2	Link 3	Discussion
(p_0, C_0)	(p_0, C_0)	(p_0, C_0)	
(p_0-1, C_0)	(p_0-1, C_0)	(p_0-1, C_0)	
...	...	...	
(p_0-k, C_0)	(p_0-k, C_0)	(p_0-k, C_0)	
$(p_0-k-1, C_0 \rightarrow C_0-3)$	(p_0-k-1, C_0)	(p_0-k-1, C_0)	Reservation of 3 units at Link 1
(p_0-k-1, C_0-3)	(p_0-k-2, C_0)	(p_0-k-2, C_0)	Price of Link 1 freezes for 3 time units
(p_0-k-1, C_0-3)	(p_0-k-3, C_0)	$(p_0-k-3, C_0 \rightarrow C_0-1)$	Reservation of 1 unit at Link 3
(p_0-k-1, C_0-3)	(p_0-k-4, C_0)	(p_0-k-3, C_0-1)	Price of Link 3 freezes for 1 time units
(p_0-k-2, C_0-3)	(p_0-k-5, C_0)	(p_0-k-4, C_0-1)	

It is proven that this policy can be configured by means of prior provider information so that the auction can attain the efficient outcome [7]. The more accurate the provider's information is, the better the auction's performance and the closer the social welfare attained is to the maximum. Also, the distributed and non-combinatorial nature of the mechanism renders MIDAS a very attractive solution for real-world networks. Finally, it is the only solution in the literature that is indeed applicable for networks of arbitrary topology. Overall, MIDAS is a fast ε-efficient solution. The efficiency loss depends on the information available a priori to the auction that can be used for the fine-tuning of the auction's price dropping policy. MIDAS relies on the distributed running of each link's auction and which can be run in polynomial time in order to determine the best allocation of the bandwidth of a network.

CONCLUSION

The rapid growth of Internet has resulted in increased need for bandwidth. At the same time, the introduction of innovative technologies, such as optical fibers, wireless and satellite links has increased the supply of bandwidth, which is now offered at lower prices. At the same time, there are parts of the network where bottlenecks exist due to cost (ocean cable links) or business strategy issues (strategic degradation of interconnection links). This chapter has presented the main issues and mechanisms of auction-based resource allocation in telecom networks.

REFERENCES

[1]   Lazar, A.; Semret N. Design and analysis of the progressive second price auction for network bandwidth sharing. *Telecommunications Systems, Special Issue on Network Economics*, 1999.

[2]   Maillé, P.; Tuffin, B. A Progressive Second Price Mechanism with a Sanction Bid from Excluded Players, *In Proc. of ICQT'03*, LNCS 2816, 332-341, Munich, 2003.

[3]   Bitsaki, M.; Stamoulis, G.D.; Courcoubetis, C. A new strategy for bidding in the network-wide progressive second price auction for bandwidth, *Proc. of CoNEXT'05*, 146-155, 2005.

[4]   Maillé, P.; Tuffin, B. Multi-bid Auctions for Bandwidth Allocation in Communication Networks. *In Proc. of IEEE Infocom 2004*, Hong Kong.

[5]   Maillé, P.; Tuffin, B. Pricing the Internet with Multi-Bid Auctions. *IEEE/ACM Transactions on Networking*, Vol. 14, Num. 5, 992-1104, 2006.

[6]   Dramitinos, M. An Auction Mechanism for Bandwidth Allocation Over Paths, *M.Sc. Thesis*, Department of Computer Science, University of Crete, 2000.

[7]   Dramitinos, M.; Stamoulis, G.D.; Courcoubetis, C. An Auction Mechanism for Allocating the Bandwidth of Networks to their Users. *Elsevier IEEE Computer Networks*, 51:18 4979-4996, December 2007.

Chapter 9

AUCTION-BASED RESOURCE RESERVATION IN WIRELESS 3G NETWORKS

ABSTRACT

Auctions have recently received considerable attention as an economic mechanism for resource reservation and price discovery in networks. This is of particular importance for many practical cases such as the provision of network services with long duration and high demand for network resources. A prominent case is that of UMTS: except for voice, the duration of services that users generally request is significantly longer than a single time slot over which resource units can be reserved; e.g., large file transfers or video streaming of a certain bit rate.

In this chapter we present a research proposal for applying an auction mechanism in the problem of resource allocation to the competing data flows of users in the context of 3G networks. Though this chapter focuses on presenting an auction for High Speed Data Packet Access (HSDPA) 3G networks, it should be emphasized that the proposed mechanism is applicable to any 2,5/3G network technology. Indeed, it suffices to change the definition of "resource units" to pertain to the respective network's resources and the auction still can be employed.

INTRODUCTION

Auctions have recently received considerable attention as an economic mechanism for resource reservation and price discovery in networks. This is of particular importance for many practical cases such as the provision of network services with long duration and high demand for network resources. A prominent case is that of UMTS [1], [2]: except for voice, the duration of services that users generally request is significantly longer than a single time slot over which resource units can be reserved; e.g., large file transfers or video streaming of a certain bit rate. These services require Quality of Service (QoS), and are very demanding in resources.

The Universal Mobile Telecommunications System (UMTS) is a third generation (3G) cellular networks technology. In particular, cellular networks emerged as second-generation (2G) technology focusing on the provision of wireless voice services to their mobile subscribers. The dominant standard of such networks is GSM. It soon became apparent that there was need to provide some data services on top of these cellular networks as well. This led to the so-called 2,5G networks, i.e. to the General Packet Radio Service (GPRS). GPRS was built on top of the circuit-switched GSM networks as a best effort packet switched service. The rates supported by GPRS, and its enhanced version EDGE, are generally low, with a maximum rate of 180kbps. On the contrary, UMTS can support high data rate services and can support QoS. This is in contrast with both the low data rates and the best effort nature of 2,5G networks.

UMTS networks use the Widepoint Code Division Multiple Access (W-CDMA) method, which prescribes that a user's voice or data service is spread over both time and frequency within a frame. The duration of the frame of a UMTS network is 10msec. Accommodating long-lived services consists a challenge for 3G networks due to the scarcity of the radio spectrum. To this end, 3GPP Release 5 defines the High Speed Downlink Packet Access (HSDPA), which provides a much faster downlink shared channel (HS-DSCH) than that of the 3GPP Release '99 [3]. This is mostly due to the different modulation used and the smaller duration of the frame, which is only 2msec.

At the end of 2008, the percentage of worldwide wireless subscriptions, which were 3G, was approximately 11%. By the end of 2013, according to recent market surveys, the percentage of 3G and 4G subscriptions is expected to increase dramatically up to 30%,. This projection is based on the current market trends that are reflected in the fourth quarter 2008 wireless infrastructure contract awards. Therefore, the 3G services market this is one of the fastest growing and highly competitive sectors of the telecoms industry.

Since the mobile industry is extremely competitive and spectrum is a scarce resource, the efficient spectrum management is crucial for commercial providers. Indeed, inefficiency (i.e. awarding the scarce network resources to those that do not value them the most) displeases the high-value users. These users may consider changing their provider, which has become easier than the past due to number portability. Hence, inefficient providers' revenue will deteriorate. Moreover, 3G spectrum is a scarce "fixed-quantity" resource, while users' demand for bandwidth is known to be exponentially increasing over time. Thus, it is crucial that efficiency is achieved.

It is worth noting that in the 3GPP requirements for Quality of Service (QoS) [4] it is emphasized that *"QoS shall support efficient resource utilization"*. Therefore, the auction must be conducted in a fixed short time scale of milliseconds so that both efficiency and fast entry of new users to the network are achieved.

An alternative to performing auctions sequentially (one per slot) would be to run combinatorial auctions, thus allowing users to bid for resources spanning several consecutive slots. Such an approach should not be adopted due to the following reasons:

i)   the computational overhead is excessive,
ii) guaranteeing resources for the entire duration of the sessions currently served would render impossible for the network to serve users with higher value (even for the same service) that would arrive late, thus resulting in high connectivity delay, poor revenue and inefficiency. Hence, this approach would ruin the social welfare attained, the incentives for rational network usage and in some cases the provider's revenue as well. An illustrative example follows.

Assume that the program of a TV channel is available through streaming by a 3G network that allows user reservations spanning several slots. Assume that this channel is currently broadcasting a highly unpopular TV show, but in a few minutes the popular Champion's League final will be broadcasted. In such a case, users have the incentive to subscribe to watching the channel's program for the next 100 minutes, while the show is broadcasted, in order to make sure that they will be able to watch the forthcoming football match. However, there might be many other users (with higher willingness to pay for the service) that shall not be admitted to the network later due to lack of resources. Thus, an approach that combines call admission control with user reservations spanning several slots results in inefficiency, low provider's revenue, displeased high-value users and lack of incentives for rational network usage by the users.

In this chapter, we present an HSDPA auction-basEd Resource Allocation mechanism (HERA).

HERA: HSDPA Auction-Based Resource Allocation

The auction mechanism proposed extends the HSDPA scheduler that is responsible for sharing the High Speed Downlink Shared Channel (HS-DSCH) among users in the time domain [10]. This scheme, henceforth referred to as HERA, conducts a sequence of mini-auctions, each concerning reservation of resources within 1 sec, or 500 frames with duration of 2 msec.

This proposed mechanism comprises: (a) a series of repeated Generalized Vickrey Auctions, one per slot, and (b) certain bidding functions for the user to choose from. The proposed auction mechanism deals with how to satisfy the demand for large time-scale services of constant bit rate (CBR), by allocating *nearly consistently* (same amount of resources over time) resources to those users that value them the most. A realistic assumption in this context is that the population of users generally varies over time, as in practical cases, which further complicates the problem.

Multicast further complicates the already difficult issue of bandwidth allocation between competing terminals, since multicast and unicast flows reflect different costs to the network and different benefits to the users. For simplicity reasons, the proposed auction only considers the downlink bandwidth allocation problem.

The primary design goal for the auction-based algorithm is to allocate the scarce network resources *efficiently*, that is, so as to maximize the social welfare attained. In addition, proper user incentives must be provided for rational network usage. This means that admission to the network should be easier and cheaper in off-peak periods, while retaining service should be harder and more costly during peak demand periods. Customers who declare a higher willingness to pay for receiving service should be *preferred* to those of mediocre willingness to pay, who are less anxious to use data services and less willing to pay for the network resources.

In order to reduce the search space for the possible auction algorithms, the following assumptions have been made:

- The primary goal of the auction is *social welfare maximization*. The secondary goals are attaining sufficient revenue for the network provider and providing good quality of service to competing unicast and multicast flows

- To minimize traffic over the Radio Access Network (RAN), the user should only submit a total willingness to pay along with each service request. Bidding should be automated and conducted in the Node B (the base station of the 3G network).
- Since radio spectrum is the scarcest resource, the auction will only be concerned with optimizing the bandwidth allocation over the wireless downlink in each cell, ignoring the landline parts of the network.
- We assume that different content variants of a single multicast flow may be delivered to different user terminals (UEs), based on either transcoding or layered coding.

Based on these assumptions, the designer of an appropriate auction algorithm has to take into account the following issues:

Efficiency versus end-to-end guarantees: In order for the auction to be efficient, it must run in a relatively short time scale that captures the market fluctuations. However, this means that no end-to-end guarantees can be provided for longer sessions.

Content variants and user demand: The availability of multiple content variants for each service means that the user should be able to submit different bids for each variant, either exclusive or summable ones, reflecting the user's different total willingness to pay for each content variant.

Bidding and perceived QoS: Since the allocation of resources by the auction depends solely on the bids submitted, it may become infeasible for a user or multicast group to continue receiving service at a certain time interval, due to network dynamics. Therefore, proper user utility functions should be defined to express the preferences of the users with respect to the resource allocation pattern when perfectly consistent allocation cannot be attained.

HERA comprises a series of *consecutive auctions* as a means for attaining efficiently consistent reservation of resources. Each auction spans a time period of 1 sec and its outcome specifies the allocation of 500 2msec HSDPA frames (see below). Each user aims in being allocated a certain quantity of frames within the 1 sec period so that his target bit rate is attained.

Economists have analyzed the repetition of auctions. Nevertheless, most of the related works focus on comparisons of sequential and simultaneous auctions and the problems that auction repetition imposes on incentive compatibility (see [5] and [6]). Closely related to the problem of consistent resource allocation in a multitude of auctions for long-lived services is that studied by Crèmer and Hariton in [7]. Crèmer and Hariton also recognize that certain Internet applications require guaranteed capacity over longer time periods than others. Thus, [7] deals analytically with the properties of a Vickrey-type mechanism for accommodating such applications' demand for a pipe.

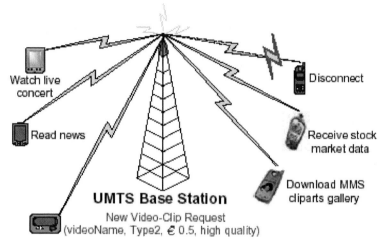

Figure 9.1. A user of a UMTS cell submits a video service request consisting of the video name, his selection of a utility function and his total willingness to pay for that service of a certain quality (bit rate).

However, the assumptions in the models analyzed in [7] are considerably different than those of HERA: It is taken that each application lasts for either one or two time slots, and that usage of the pipe is dedicated entirely to a single application (as opposed to being shared at portions to be determined) by means of a Vickrey-type auction in which at most two users participate. Under these assumptions, the authors of [7] analyze the users' bidding strategies, the revenues associated with the auction mechanism, and for a special case they derive the optimal revenues. Hence, Crèmer and Hariton do not attempt to address the issue of designing a suitable auction mechanism for long-lived user services over a wireless network.

Each mini-auction of the HERA mechanism is a sealed-bid Generalized Vickrey Auction (GVA) [8], with *atomic bids*, i.e. bids that are either fully satisfied or rejected. The bids have the form (p, q), where q is the quantity of resource units (2 msec frames) sought in the present auction and p is the proposed price for each unit. After the placement of all users' bids, the frames are allocated to the highest bids and each user is charged according to the social opportunity cost that his presence entails, which is less than his declared willingness to pay [8]. This means that each user pays the auction bids of others that would have become winning in the auction if his own bids were set to zero; hence his charge for receiving service is less than his declared willingness to pay for the service.

The time period of the auction t_a, was set to 1 sec so that it is both small enough to capture market fluctuations due to mobility and large enough to accommodate diverse bit-rate requests. As a result, the minimum bit-rate (denoted as R_{min}) that can be awarded by the auction (a single 2 msec frame in 1 sec) is approximately 20 Kbps or 1,33 Kbps, depending on whether the HS-DSCH frame is configured to contain 1 or 15 codes, respectively. This provides very fine granularity in the set of achievable bit-rates: if the desired bit-rate for a service is m, we simply set $q = m / R_{min}$. This way, the exclusive use of the High Speed Downlink Shared CHannel (suggested in [10]) is also possible, as long as the RNC configuration defines that the number of HS-DSCH codes per frame is set to 1.

However, in a realistic case of a UMTS network, it is not feasible for users to participate in all these mini-auctions, either manually or automatically by means of an agent running in their respective terminal. Thus, since the user cannot give his utility on a per mini-auction basis, we define meaningful utility functions, pertaining to the various services. These functions are provided by the network operator for the user to choose from and scaled by the user's total willingness to pay, which is to be given by the user himself (as part of his service request). This is similar to the 3GPP's approach [4] about predefined QoS profiles. Then, the network runs all mini-auctions by bidding optimally for each of the users, according to his respective selection of utility function. Thus, *all computation is performed on the network base stations rather than on the user terminals*. The network and auction complexity are hidden from the users: A user demanding a service selects among the predefined utility functions the one that better expresses his preferences and declares a willingness to pay U_s; a session that lasts for time t_s is then created. Each user aims in achieving constantly the desired rate m_i by bidding in a large number K_s of mini-auctions (Recall, however, the network is bidding on each user's behalf).

This agrees with the 3GPP requirement [4] that "QoS behavior should be dynamic, i.e. it shall be possible to modify QoS parameters during an active session". If the user wishes to watch his favorite music video clip lasting for 4 minutes, all that he declares is the video name, a total willingness to pay U_s, the desired quality level, and the utility function type, as shown in Figure 1.

The rest parameters are computed automatically by the network and are transparent to the user.

Thus, our auction-based mechanism comprises three layers: a) the Service Layer, where users request services; b) the Auction Layer where user-supplied information is mapped to auction-specific parameters and resources are allocated by means of auctions; and c) the Network Layer where the allocated resources are actually reserved.

HERA User Utility Functions

This subsection presents the user utility functions, pertaining to the various services, as well as the "sub-utility" and "sub-bidding" functions for each "mini-auction", since the declaration of the user's total (maximum) willingness to pay for the service is allowed once per *session*. The latter must be computed in a meaningful way according to the user's utility function and have nice properties regarding incentive compatibility. Instead of letting the users declare such functions, the network uses predefined such functions, one per service, and computes the bidding function optimally for users, thus aiming to maximize their net benefit. These utility functions are scaled by the user's total (maximum) willingness to pay $U_{s,i}$, provided by the user as part of his service request. The network then runs the various mini-auctions by bidding on behalf of each user, according to his selection of bidding function. To be more precise, at each mini-auction t, the network bids on behalf of the user the subutility $v_{s,i}^{(t)}(x_i^{(1)}, ..., x_i^{(t)})$ that would be attained if the user were indeed winner in this auction. This subutility depends on the selection of a utility function and is defined later in this section for various types of users.

We will now present the utility functions that we have designed and their properties. We assume that the total value $u_{s,i}$ from obtaining the service s for user i (that is a quantification of the user-perceived QoS) is the sum of the marginal sub-utilities attained by the user due to each successful allocation, that is:

$$u_{s,i}(x_i^{(1)}, ..., x_i^{(Ks,i)}) = \sum_{t=1}^{Ks,i} v_{s,i}^{(t)}(x_i^{(1)}, ..., x_i^{(t)})$$

$K_{s,i}$ denotes the number of mini-auctions that user i participates in during service s, t indicates the current mini-auction and $v_{s,i}$ denotes the marginal sub-utility attained during the each auction, which we will define below for each type of service. The utility functions that we have designed reflect the fact that when there are gaps in the resource allocation pattern, not only the amount of allocated slots but also the way these are allocated makes a difference, possibly considerable, to the degree of user satisfaction. By selecting one of the predefined user utility functions, each user declares his preferred allocation pattern when perfectly consistent resource reservation is not possible. In particular, we have defined the following utility functions:

Type 1: Indifferent to the allocation pattern. This type pertains to volume-oriented users, such as those downloading news articles. The utility depends only on the quantity allocated, as opposed to the allocation pattern, hence,

$$v_{s,i}^{(t)}(x_i^{(1)},..., x_i^{(t)}) = 1(x_i^{(t)} = m_i) \cdot \frac{U_{s,i}}{K_{s,i}},$$

where $U_{s,i}$ is the user's declared total willingness-to-pay and $1(.)$ is the indicator function.

Therefore, the lack of information transfer due to the gaps in the resource allocation pattern, results in proportional loss of user satisfaction. As already mentioned, an appropriate example of users belonging to this type is that of users accessing news with a certain target bit rate. Also, users downloading information by means of FTP can be considered as users of this type, provided that the FTP session is capable of resuming download when time-outs occur. This utility function is suitable for the UMTS Background Class services with m_i pertaining to the Maximum Bit-rate parameter of this class [4]. Note that since users are "volume-oriented", a rate less than m_i would also be useful to them. That is, if a user has the last winning bid and he can be awarded just a fraction of the target bit rate, it is both meaningful and efficient to do so. This can be attained if the assumption of atomic bids is relaxed. On the contrary, it is obviously inefficient to assign to the higher value users a bit rate less than their maximum.

Type 2: *Sensitive to service continuity.* This type pertains to users that prefer watching consistently half of a football match rather than watching multiple shorter periods.

Thus, they prefer the allocation pattern of Figure 9.2(a) to that of Figure 9.2(b), hence $v_{s,i}^{(t)}(x_i^{(1)},..., x_i^{(t)}) = 1(x_i^{(t)} = m_i) \cdot \dfrac{U_{s,i}}{K_{s,i}} \cdot \alpha^{d_i}$, $0 < \alpha < 1$, where d_i is the distance between the current and the previous slots during which user i achieved reservations. The previous allocations influence $v_{s,i}^{(t)}$ and thus the user's subsequent bid through d_i, which is tracked by the Node B (or the RNC). This utility function is suitable for the UMTS streaming class.

Type 3: Sensitive to service regularity. This type pertains to users that prefer the allocation pattern of Figure 9.2(b) to that of Figure 9.2(a). The corresponding sub-utility is

$$v_{s,i}^{(t)}(x_i^{(1)},..., x_i^{(t)}) = 1(x_i^{(t)} = m_i) \cdot \dfrac{U_{s,i}}{K_{s,i}} \cdot \alpha^{\max\{0,\Delta d_i\}}, \quad \text{where} \quad \Delta d_i \quad \text{is the}$$

difference of d_i (as defined above) and the size of the previous such gap. Note that the factor $\alpha^{\max\{0,\Delta d_i\}}$ equals 1 if Δd_i is negative, that is, the distance decreases or remains constant, i.e. quality improves or remains stable, and is less than 1 if the distance increases, i.e. quality deteriorates. This utility function is also suitable for the UMTS streaming class.

For all three types, if the user is constantly allocated resources the utility obtained is $U_{s,i}$. So far, we have implicitly assumed unicast flows and thus individual users' willingness to pay. However, there exists the MBMS subsystem of 3G networks, which is used for the delivery of such data services and can also accomodate multicast flows. In order to accommodate this in our model, it suffices for multicast flows to use $U_{s,i}$ to denote *the sum of* the total willingness to pay declared by each member of the multicast group.

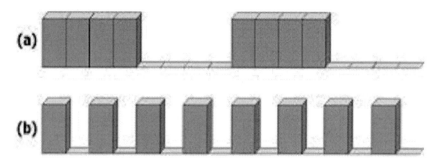

Figure 9.2. Different resource allocation patterns.

USER INCENTIVES

We briefly address the issue of user incentives for this repeated game, where users bid in a sequence of auctions.

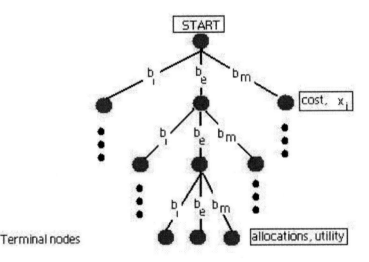

Figure 9.3. The sequential from of the fame for a user bidding in 3 auctions.

Node START denotes user's i start of bidding and in general each node (*state*) corresponds to the bidding phase of each auction he participates. At each node user i selects an *action*, i.e. to bid truthfully $b_e = w_i$, or shade his bid $b_l < w_i$, or bid aggressively $b_m > w_i$, with w_i denoting the user's willingness to pay. It is easy to show that incentive compatibility holds if user bids for independent services at the various auctions.

We then address the most interesting case where *complementarities* exist among the user allocations in subsequent auctions, i.e. when the user receives a long-lived service and has to bid in a sequence of auctions: Placing a bid b_l at any auction is not beneficial, since b_l only increases the probability of losing without affecting the payment.

It could be argued however that a bid b_m can be beneficial, due to the extra value that a present allocation (which becomes more likely by over-bidding) can bring to the overall service. However, it can be proved that this would *not* be the case for extremely "uncertainty averse" (conservative) users, who - by definition - in cases of choice/behavior under *uncertainty* always opt to play the safest strategy. Therefore, for this type of users truthful bidding comprises a subgame perfect equilibrium strategy. This "maximin" behavior was proposed by Wald [13] for situations of severe uncertainty, which is also encountered by the bidders of the HERA auction.

Note that adopting such an overbidding strategy exposes the user to the risk of being awarded slots that bring negative net benefit due to the overbidding.

For example, this might be the case if he overbids for the last slot won, or if he overbids too much for a slot (pays more money than the extra net benefit the allocation of the slot results in the allocation pattern). Though it is not feasible for a bidder to estimate how probable this may be, the important thing is that there is positive probability that this might actually happen.

This where the argument about uncertainty averse bidders due to the complete lack of information, comes handy: These bidders play the "maximin" strategy, thus in our case they always place a bid b_e.

This argument has been used elsewhere in economics. Except from Wald [13], [15], [16], [17] and [18] also use a similar approach. In fact, a thorough discussion on the maximin behavior is included in [17]. Note that the above behavior is also applicable to games of partial information where the set of *beliefs* for rival players' strategies might be wrong (such as [19], [20]).

In such cases, the maximization of a Von Neumann-Morgenstern utility function is not enough for extremely uncertainty averse - i.e. conservative - bidders who prefer to sacrifice some potential payoff for more security in an uncertain environment. In our case, the worst outcome is that the slot's cost - due to the overbidding - will be finally higher than the extra value it brings to the successive slots awarded.

A complete incentives analysis and proof can be found in [10].

EXPERIMENTAL ASSESSMENT

This subsection presents an evaluation of the HERA mechanism by means of auction. In particular, it is investigated whether users can get indeed satisfactory service by means of this automated bidding in a large series of auctions. We also assess the impact of multicast and examine whether an alternative not economic-aware allocation mechanism/scheduling policy could have been adopted and its comparative performance with respect to that of HERA.

Resource Allocation Patterns

A plethora of simulations confirms that when a user's bids are always higher (lower) than each mini-auction's lowest winning bid (the cut-off price), then the allocation pattern was perfectly consistent (the user was allocated no resources at all). Simulations have also revealed the following property of the auction scheme: the vast majority of the users' resource allocation patterns are either nearly consistent or represent very low quantities of resources. The congestion level of the network, that is, the total demand for resources, affects the percentage of the users receiving very satisfactory service. However, the congestion level has very limited effect on the aforementioned bi-modal distribution of the resource allocation patterns, and intermediate allocation patterns arise rarely in general. Hence, HERA serves as a "soft" call admission control mechanism, blocking users with non-competitive total willingness to pay from receiving service by the network and leading to nearly consistent allocation for the competitive users.

The impact of multicast costs on the revenue and social welfare attained has also been investigated in [21]. This issue is considered to be significant, since it may determine whether multicast services will be attractive for commercial networks.

The key findings are:

- Social welfare is substantially improved if multicast is employed, due to the larger amount of users that are served by the network. The higher the number of multicast sessions served, the higher the improvement of social welfare compared to that attained by unicast.
- The impact on social welfare and revenue depends on the level of competition and *both* the *cost* of multicast sessions and the *size* of the multicast groups.
- The assumption that multicast sessions cost more than unicast ones in terms of resources reduces the effect of demand reduction that the resource aggregation inherent in multicast implies, thus improving revenue. Moreover, when this cost becomes high it might actually stimulate competition even with medium to low demand for resources.
- The higher the cost of the multicast sessions, the more difficult it becomes for multicast users with a low willingness to pay to compete against unicast users with high willingness to pay. The probability of winning in such settings under various levels of competition (i.e.

demand for resources) is severely affected by the size of the multicast groups.

The fact that social welfare is always improved by employing multicast was something to be expected. In general, the quantity of resources required by a multicast group is less than the sum of resources of the same users when served with unicast, if the group size is over a certain threshold. Therefore, a higher number of users will be admitted to the network, since resources have a higher degree of utilization, thus increasing the number of the auction winners and the respective sum of users' utilities that are served by the network, which is the social welfare.

Unlike with social welfare, the impact of multicast on provider's revenue is not trivial. Indeed, a common myth supports that since multicast reduces the cut-off price, and thus the social opportunity cost, under any usage-based pricing-scheme (including auctions), a network provider is always better off if only unicast flows are admitted to his network as multicast flows will necessarily reduce revenues. However, our analysis indicates that this is not always the case.

The main reason for this phenomenon is the wealth asymmetry of the bidders. In high competition, users with low or medium willingness to pay rarely win some auctions, or can afford to pay the dynamic price that is determined by balancing demand and supply under other usage based pricing schemes. Hence, these users have no chance of either winning or affecting the prices, simply because their bids are the lowest. Therefore, competition takes place only among a subset of users, those having a high willingness to pay; these are declared either winners or losers and their bids determine the social opportunity cost for the winners. Multicast however enables "low-value" users to build groups (where even users with high willingness to pay may join) thus submitting competitive bids in the auction. Therefore, users that had no chance of affecting the auction outcome may now participate in bids that are high enough to either a) become winning and displace some high value unicast bidders whose bids will increase the social opportunity cost that winners pay or b) become losing just below the cut-off auction price, thus raising the charges for the winners.

Indeed, when competition is medium and the wealth asymmetry of the bidders is limited, the revenue attained when multicast is employed though higher, is very close to that attained if no multicast sessions are allowed. However, introducing wealth asymmetry (low-value users form groups while high-value compete individually as unicast) results in higher gains for the provider in terms of revenue. The social welfare in both cases is significantly improved when multicast is employed and heavily dependent on the probability of the multicast sessions to be served by the network. In contrast, in case of low competition, there is significant reduction in revenue; employing multicast in this case results in eliminating the competition in the auction.

Comparative assessment of HERA, Round Robin and FCFS

This chapter has so far presented an auction-based mechanism for resource reservation in 3G networks and assessed some of its properties. An interesting question is whether things would be better or worse if an alternative resource allocation policy had been adopted. This is investigated in the remainder of this subsection, where a comparative assessment of HERA with some well-known scheduling policies is presented, namely the Round Robin and the First Come First Served policies.

Round Robin prescribes that at every moment in time, the available resources are shared equally among the users/processes demanding them. Formally, a round robin schedule is an arrangement of repeatedly choosing all elements in a group equally in some rational order, i.e. round robin is about "taking turns". In the context of this research approach, focus is placed on accommodating user services that demand certain quantities of network resources for partly overlapping different time intervals. It is worth noting that employing the Round Robin algorithm in this context implies that users receive the quantity of resources they demand one after another; after all of them have been served, this process is repeated.

First Come First Served is a service policy whereby the requests of customers are attended to in the order that they arrive, without any other criteria. In our context, employing this algorithm implies that user sessions are served according to the ordering of the user sessions' arrival time. It is worth noting that it is possible that a user arriving at time t to need to wait until time $t' > t$ to be served. This occurs in cases where there are not enough network resources available to serve both this session and those that arrived at times prior to t. Thus, user sessions are "shifted" in time until the network can admit and serve them. In the simulations conducted, we do not allow the waiting user sessions to depart from the system, unless the respective session length of the session exceeds the number of the remaining slots of the simulation; i.e. for a simulation of 5000 slots, a user demanding service for 300 slots will depart from the system at slot 4701, provided that he has not been served yet. This typically happens in case the competition is high and the user's arrival time is towards the end of the simulation time.

It is also worth emphasizing that under the FCFS scheme, users either receive service with perfect quality or are not served at all. Note however that the waiting time of the users that are served may be arbitrarily high.

Next, some experimental results depicting the different performance of these schemes are presented.

The first experiment regards resource allocation for 500 slots, and is typical of the mechanisms' performance under *weak competition*. In particular, there are 10 low-value Type 1 users, 15 high-value Type 2 users and 15 high-value Type 3 users. Figure 9.4 depicts the distribution of user resource allocation patterns. It can be seen that due to the low competition (demand marginally exceeds supply) all three mechanisms result in very good quality for the users – most of them reserve 100% of the resources demanded – and that even Round Robin awards efficiently the network resources. Note that under the auction mechanism and the FCFS policy, two and one users respectively do not receive service at all, while the rest receive service of very good or perfect quality. As already explained, under FCFS all users that are admitted in the network receive service of perfect quality. However, some of them experience some delay prior to start receiving service. The non-zero delay that 7 users experience prior to start being serviced, as well as the average delay is depicted in Figure 9.5.

The second experiment regards resource allocation for 500 slots, and is typical of the mechanisms' performance under *medium competition*. In particular, there are 10 low-value Type 1 users, 25 high-value Type 2 users and 25 high-value Type 3 users. Figure 9.6 depicts the distribution of user resource allocation patterns. It can be seen that due to the medium competition (demand exceeds supply) Round Robin's performance is rather bad compared to the previous case.

Indeed, due to the relatively increased competition, more intermediate resource allocation patterns arise. Note however, that this is not the case for our auction competition, whose performance is similar to that of the FCFS. Indeed, under both the auction and the FCFS mechanisms, the number of users that attain perfect or close to perfect quality comes very close; the same applies for the number of users who are not essentially served.

Obviously, under the auction mechanism there are few intermediate resource allocation patterns – that under the FCFS correspond to users who are not served at all. This is due to the fact that users that cannot be served perfectly under FCFS are not served at all, while no such provision is made for the auction.

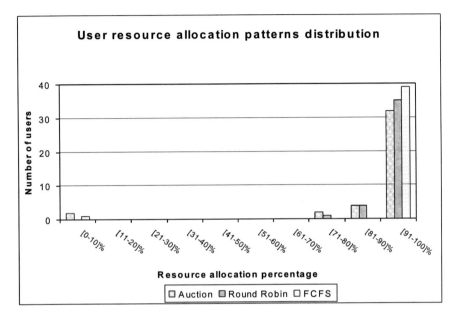

Figure 9.4. Distribution of user resource allocation patterns in a typical experiment of low competition.

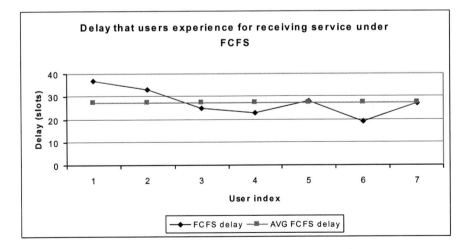

Figure 9.5. Delay that users experience for receiving service under FCFS when competition is low.

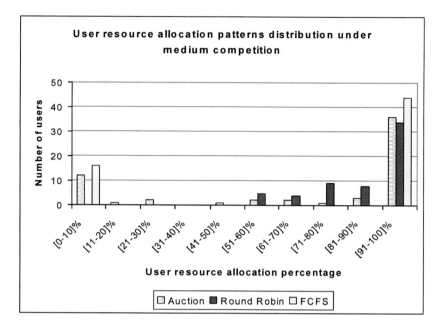

Figure 9.6. Distribution of user resource allocation patterns in a typical experiment of low competition.

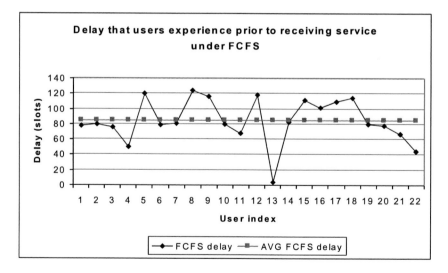

Figure 9.7. Delay that users experience for receiving service under FCFS when competition is medium.

However, under the auction mechanisms, it is always true that the low-value users are not served, while this is not the case under FCFS, since FCFS makes this decision by examining solely the user arrival slot. Last but not least, under the auction users do not suffer any delay prior to start receiving service; if they cannot be served they are not "shifted" in time, as is the case for FCFS, thus also increasing the probability of appearance of "intermediate" resource allocation patterns.

As already explained, under FCFS all users that are admitted in the network receive service of perfect quality. However, some of them experience some delay prior to start receiving service. The non-zero delay that 22 users experience prior to start being serviced, as well as the average delay in this experiment is depicted in Figure 9.7. It is worth noting that compared to the previous experiments, more users suffer delays (22) and the values of these delays as well as their average are much higher.

The third experiment regards resource allocation for 500 slots, and is typical of the mechanisms' performance under high competition. In particular, there are 10 low-value Type 1 users, 35 high-value Type 2 users and 35 high-value Type 3 users. Figure 9.8 depicts the distribution of user resource allocation patterns. It is seen that due to the high competition (demand significantly exceeds supply), Round Robin's performance is very low, and many intermediate user resource allocation patterns appear when this mechanism is employed. This is to be expected, since Round Robin by trying to perform a "balanced" allocation of resources under high competition only manages to create a significant amount of intermediate users. The higher the number of slots the experiment is run for and the higher the competition, the worse the performance of the Round Robin becomes. Indeed, under high competition Round Robin can only provide perfectly consistent resource allocation patterns in epochs where the demand is less than the supply.

Note however, that this is not the case for the HERA mechanism, whose performance is once more close to that of the FCFS. Indeed, under both the auction and the FCFS mechanisms, the probability of appearance of "intermediate" resource allocation patterns is small. The better behavior of FCFS is once more justified by the "time shifting" performed for the user sessions under FCFS and the fact that these leave the network when they cannot be served perfectly.

The non-zero delay that 34 users experience prior to start being serviced, as well as the average delay in this experiment is depicted in Figure 9.9. It is worth noting that compared to the previous experiments, more users suffer delays (34) and the values of these delays as well as their average are much higher. The higher the competition, the more intense this is.

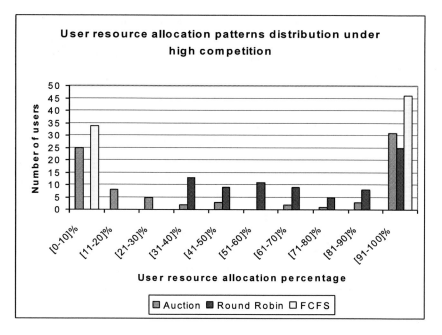

Figure 9.8. Distribution of user resource allocation patterns in a typical experiment of low competition.

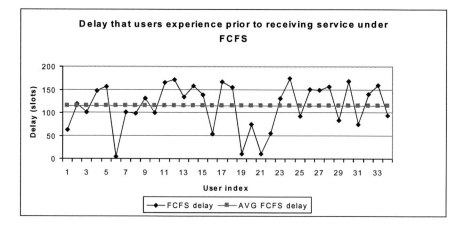

Figure 9.9. Delay that users experience for receiving service under FCFS when competition is high.

From the experimental analysis provided above, it can be seen that for various levels of competition the HERA auction mechanism results in "binary" distribution of resource allocation patterns: under HERA, competitive users receive service of very good quality and are charged according to demand, and non-competitive users are not essentially served while paying a very low or zero charge; also, intermediate patterns with a significant but unsatisfactory amount of resources and a non-negligible charge arise rarely. Thus, our resource reservation mechanism serves as soft CAC.

On the contrary, this property does not apply for the Round Robin policy. Indeed, the more intense the competition, the worse Round Robin performs. As expected, FCFS results in serving more users with perfect quality than those under our auction mechanism, due to the "time shifting" performed under this policy and the fact that we have opted that a user is served only if it is guaranteed that he will receive perfect quality of service.

Note however that the users under FCFS have to wait prior to start receiving service, for periods that becomes arbitrarily high as competition increase. Therefore, in a realistic 3G network, most of these users – that appear in the aforementioned charts as being served with perfect QoS – would leave the network.

Clearly, the auction mechanism we propose does not suffer from this problem. There is a small sacrifice in the perceived quality of service for some users, which is compensated by the fact that many users are admitted in the network and served satisfactorily.

It is also worth taking into account that FCFS serves users regardless of their respective willingness to pay, based only on their arrival time in the network. Therefore, under this scheme, the users have no means of expressing their urgency of receiving service. On the contrary, our auction-based mechanism enables users to express their willingness to pay, thus improving the social welfare attained and enabling 3G networks to serve their high value customers.

Overall, this experimental assessment indicates that the HERA auction-based mechanism is preferable to both Round Robin, since the latter produces many intermediate user resource allocation patterns. It is also a better solution than employing FCFS, since the latter results in unacceptably high session set up delays and does not take into account the social welfare attained, while the number of users served is close to the number of successfully served users under our auction-based mechanism.

MAPPING HERA TO DIFFERENT TRANSMISSION TECHNOLOGIES

So far, when describing the operation of HERA we used the terms "units" of allocation (e.g. bits) and "slots" (e.g. time-slots) in order to keep the presentation as general as possible. In this chapter, we have used the 2ms HSDPA slots as the unit of allocation. In this subsection, we define the "units" of allocation, the "slots" of the Network Layer of our auction-based resource reservation mechanism for a variety of network technologies.

The 10 msec WCDMA frame is used by the UTRAN in UMTS. This frame constitutes the allocation slot when units of resources are allocated in bits over the Downlink Shared Channel (DSCH). UMTS supports the concept of allocating Bandwidth on Demand (BoD). The entity that allocates the network resources within each frame among the users is the resource manager.

The HERA mechanism is also applicable to GPRS and its enhanced version EDGE. In GPRS, user data services compete for a number of time slots, with the unit of allocation being the radio block. Users attempt to reserve resources in order to accommodate their large time scale traffic; this traffic is transferred in bursts, by means of Temporary Block Flows within the PDP context, as described in [12].

Finally, in MBMS the "units" of allocation are analogous to that of the underlying UMTS network, i.e. the number of bits transferred over the physical channels of the RAN.

It is worth noting that since the auction and the physical layer of the auction-based framework are independent, the proposed mechanism is general enough to be employed with a variety of network technologies, as long as there is an entity controlling access to the radio spectrum (i.e. the Base Station or Node B). The only modification needed in order to employ the auction in a different network technology is to define a different "mapping" of the auction terms to actual network resources (e.g. bits, power) and, possibly, fine-tuning of the auction parameters (e.g. the auction frequency depends on the duration of the "slots" that each network provides).

CONCLUSION

In this chapter we presented HERA, an effective auction-based mechanism for the UMTS High Speed Downlink Packet Access (HSDPA).

The mechanism can deal successfully with long time-scale data, audio and video services in practical cases of networks with large numbers of competing users. It is based on a series of Generalized Vickrey Auctions and a set of user utility functions expressing the user's preferences with respect to the resource allocation patterns. Though this chapter focuses on presenting an auction for HSDPA, which is the "business logic" of the HSDPA scheduler, it should be emphasized that the proposed mechanism is applicable to any 2.5/3G network technology. Indeed, it suffices to change the definition of "resource units" to pertain to the respective network's resources and the auction still can be employed. The respective mapping of "units" to actual network resources for GPRS and UMTS Downlink Shared Channel are provided as Appendix. Overall, this research proposal is highly promising for applying auction based resource allocation schemes in the context of 3G and 4G wireless networks.

REFERENCES

[1]   Holma, H.; Toskala, A. WCDMA for UMTS: Radio Access for Third Generation Mobile Communications; John Wiley: New York, NY, 2000; ISBN 0-471-72051-8.

[2]   3GPP, URL: http://www.3gpp.org/.

[3]   Holma, H.; Toskala, A. Third Generation WCDMA radio evolution. *Wireless Communications and Mobile Computing*, 3, 978-992, 2003.

[4]   3GPP, Technical Specification Group Services and System Aspects, QoS Concept (3G TR 23.107 version 5.6.0), URL: http://www.3 gpp.org/.

[5]   Dow, J.; da Costa Werlang, S. R. Uncertainty Aversion, Risk Aversion, and the Optimal Choice of Portfolio. *Econometrica*, 60:1, 197-204, January 1992.

[6]   Friedman, D. Evolutionary Games in Economics. *Econometrica*, 59:3, 637-666, May 1991.

[7]   Crèmer, J.; Hariton, C. The pricing of critical applications in the Internet, *Journal of the Japanese and International Economies*, 13:4. 281-310, December 1999.

[8]   Courcoubetis, C.; Weber, R. *Pricing Communication Networks: Economics, Technology and Modelling*, Wiley and Sons, 2003, ISBN 0-470-85130-9.

[9]   Krishna, V. *Auction Theory*, Academic Press, April 2002, ISBN 0-12426297-X.

[10] Dramitinos, M.; Stamoulis, G.D.; Courcoubetis, C. Auction-based Resource Allocation in UMTS High Speed Downlink Packet Access, *In Proc. of First EuroNGI Conference on Traffic Engineering [NGI 2005]*, pp. 434-441, Rome, Italy, April 2005.

[11] Frodigh, M.; Parkvall, S.; Roobol, C.; Johansson, P.; Larsson, P. "Future-Generation Wireless Networks", *IEEE Personal Communications*, 8(5), 10-17, October 2001.

[12] Soursos, S.; Courcoubetis, C.; Polyzos, G.C. Differentiated Services in the GPRS Wireless Access Environment, *Proc. of the 2001 Tyrrhenian International Workshop on Digital Communications, IWDC* 2001, Evolutionary Trends of the Internet, September 17-20, 2001, Italy.

[13] Wald, A. *Statistical Decision Functions*, New York: John Wiley, 1950.

[14] Dow, J.; da Costa Werlang, S. R. Uncertainty Aversion, Risk Aversion, and the Optimal Choice of Portfolio, *Econometrica*, 60:1, 197-204, January 1992.

[15] Ellsberg, D. Risk, Ambiguity and the Savage Axioms. *The Quarterly Journal of Economics*, 75:4, 643-669, November 1961.

[16] Rawls, J. *A Theory of Justice*, Cambridge: Harvard University Press, 1971.

[17] Rawls, J. Some Reasons for the Maximin Criterion. The American Economic Review, Papers and Proceedings of the Eighty-sixth Annual Meeting of the American Economic Association, 64:2, 141-146, May 1974.

[18] Simonsen, Rational Expectations, Income Policies and Game Theory. *Revista de Econometria*, 6, 7-46, 1986.

[19] Epstein, L.; Wang, T. Beliefs about Beliefs without Probabilities. *Econometrica*, 64:6, 1343-1373, November 1996.

[20] Yaari, M. The Dual Theory of Choice under Risk. *Econometrica*, 55:1, 95-115, January 1987.

[21] Dramitinos, M.; Stamoulis, G.D.; Courcoubetis, C. Auction-based Resource Reservation in 3G Networks Serving Multicast, *In Proc. of the 15th IST Mobile Summit*, Myconos, Greece, June 4-8, 2006.

[22] Friedman, D. Evolutionary Games in Economics, *Econometrica*, 59:3, 637-666, May 1991.

Chapter 10

CONCLUSION

Recent trends in telecoms, driven both by the emerging technologies and the new business models of the telecoms sector, advocate in favor of dynamic resource allocation schemes. To this end, auctions appear as a promising solution to many practical problems of resource allocation and management in present communication networks, as well as those that are expected to emerge in the coming years. This book has presented some topics where auction-based mechanisms are widely used in the telecoms sector. This has been completed with a discussion of theoretical studies that demonstrate the applicability of auction mechanisms as the basis of incentive-compatible and fair consumption of network resources.

In particular, it has been shown that auction-based allocation of spectrum licenses has become the dominant practice for many countries. There is a plethora of such auctions run in most countries of the world for the allocation of wireless spectrum licenses. The advent of new technologies such as WiMax and the world-scale transition from analogue to digital TV broadcasting will further intensify this trend. The advent of new disruptive technologies such as the Cognitive Radio Networks where idle spectrum can be dynamically accessed in an opportunistic way, without restrictions regarding the frequency bands where it is located, is a novel concept that could further advocate in favor of dynamic resource allocation mechanisms and schemes capable of operating efficiently also in fast time scales, such as auction mechanisms.

Wireless networks are the prominent candidates where such schemes could appear. The main reason for that is the scarcity of the radio spectrum, which combined with the impressive growth of end users terminals and the increased needs for more bandwidth-hungry and services demanding quality assurance, render over-provisioning a luxury. Multimedia messages (MMS) replace the short text messages (SMS), while voice calls must still be accommodated along with data (e.g. photo, video, file transfers) services of much higher data rates. Moreover, the duration of these services is orders of magnitude larger than that of the network slots where resources are allocated (e.g. the duration of a UMTS frame is 10 msec). The future convergence of the aforementioned technologies with other mobile network technologies and the potential introduction of multicast services also contribute to the dynamic nature of the telecommunications environment.

On the other hand, applying a dynamic auction scheme, like the one presented in Chapter 9, means that for some users the service may be interrupted if their bids are no longer competitive. Despite the fact that this probability can be minimized by means of careful design, this can never be zero. This appears to be the most important drawback of such schemes, which mitigates their applicability as long as the demand is in general less than the supply of network resources over time. The increasing number of mobile devices and services deployed in wireless networks indicate that taking difficult decisions that will allow the efficient utilization of spectrum and its allocation by means of economic principles is not long to come.

But what about fixed topology networks that are still overdimensioned for both performance and fault-tolerance reasons? The existing business models heavily depend on the best-effort paradigm. End-to-end quality assurance is currently only obtained by services operating below the Internet level (e.g. leased lines and Virtual Private Networks), or approximated by placing caching platforms in core networks (e.g. Akamai) if applicable. Offering better than best-effort services at the inter-domain level - a potential additional source of income for the network carriers whose profit margins are constantly declining - is not a sustainable business model in today's Internet for services spanning across multiple domains.

Also, the "traditional" strategy of overprovisioning cannot be applied in the interdomain context since there are bottlenecks such as the interconnection peering points, due to business issues. Through "selective degradation" of interconnection quality, large network carriers can prohibit the expansion of smaller networks and increase their market share. Thus, existing business models can result in significant entry barriers for new operators, who may not be recognized as "peers" by their competing networks, thus further increasing the market entry barriers and mitigating competition.

Furthermore, the exponential growth of multimedia traffic and the always-on paradigm of new devices (smartphones, iPad, etc), result in exponentially growing demand of bandwidth whose cost is substantial for the network carriers. At the same time, the popular services of Over-The-Top Providers, such as Google's YouTube, do not result in additional income for the networks that need to exercise more effort in accommodating those new demanding services, while not being directly rewarded for their effort. The Internet connectivity market exhibits information asymmetries that cause inefficiency: Network providers control all the characteristics of their networks (e.g. capacity or usage) and may or may not disclose this information to potential interconnection partners.

Current interconnection agreements do not provide economic incentives for partners to collaborate on exploiting positive network externalities. A variety of studies have demonstrated that there are significant free-riding and unfair revenue sharing issues that prohibit the investments for improving the network infrastructure and the service quality provisioned.

Overall, despite the many advantages of the simple network, the current business models also result in unmet market needs for:

- *End-users*: Users deal with the unpredictable behavior of the best-effort services offered and there is no *choice* for premium-quality services despite the relevant need. Unrealiable and unpredictable QoS levels often result in more effortful supplementary solutions, which can be considered as related external effect.
- *Network operators*: No differentiation of the network performance based on how users value different services and Quality of Experience (QoE). Provisioning QoS-sensitive services at the inter-domain level may not be sustainable under the present business models, although bilateral attempts are reported.
- *Over-The-Top Providers*: They create positive and negative externalities, due to the added value of their services and costs and overheads they give rise to. The lack of inter-domain premium network transport capabilities affects their business for certain applications with high requirements.

This motivates the need for providing sustainable business models and economic incentives and mechanisms that will be sustainable and allow the provision of better services in the interdomain level. Auction-based mechanisms that could be applied in the interdomain core for providing better than simple connectivity services starts to emerge as an attractive option for network operators. This trend is further enhanced by the emergence of new technologies such as the Grid, Service Oriented Architectures and Software on

Demand that require both virtualization and innovative resource allocation and management mechanisms.

Obviously, there are also open important technical issues that need to be solved before such auction-based mechanisms appear in the Internet (interdomain) market: The scalable and efficient creation, advertisement, management and trading of interconnection "contracts" that provide QoS assurance have not been addressed satisfactorily. Creating scalable protocols for these issues is a non-trivial issue. Going beyond the simple connectivity graph of the Border Gateway Protocol towards a both QoS- and economics-aware route selection and also enforcing QoS-routing in the underlying heterogeneous networks in the interdomain context is an open issue. This also contains an interesting set of related issues such as automated SLS negotiation, end-to-end monitoring and Service Level Agreement enforcement, revenue and penalties sharing. All these issues are within the scope of multiple research efforts that address these issues in a holistic manner, addressing both the technical and the economic aspects of these issues.

Overall, it is clear that auction theory has lots to offer in the telecoms industry in the years to come. After an impressive start with the FCC auctions, applying auction theory in the telecoms sector is yet to reach its full potential and new exciting developments are expected in the coming years.

INDEX

C

W

Y